Grown & Gone

*Stories and Tips to Help You Survive Your
First Independent Year of College*

A Series of Contributors

Grown &

Gone

Stories and Tips to Help You Survive Your
First Independent Year of College

A Series of Contributors

Impact Learning Publications

Grown & Gone
Stories and tips to help you survive your first independent year of college
Copyright © 2017 LEAD of MS, Corp.

Impact Learning Publications
PO Box 736
Tougaloo, MS 39174
www.ilpublications.com

Limit of Liability/Disclaimer of Warranty:
This book is presented solely for educational and informational purposes. The author, coauthors, and publisher are not offering it as legal or professional services advice. While best efforts have been used in preparing this book, the author, coauthors, and publisher make no representation or warranties of any kind and assume no liabilities of any kind with respect to the accuracy or completeness of the contents and specifically disclaim any implied warranties of merchantability or fitness of use for a particular purpose. Neither the author, the coauthors, the contributors, nor the publisher shall be held liable or responsible for any person or entity with respect to any loss or incidental or consequential damages caused, or alleged to have been caused, directly or indirectly, by the information or programs contained herein. No warranty may be created or extended by sales representatives or written sales materials. This information is not intended as professional advice, as professional advice has to be tailored to the specific circumstances and facts of each situation. Consult a professional before taking any action based on information contained here. Also, keep in mind that laws and practices vary from state to state. Any stories, characters, or entities contained in this work may be fictional. Any likeness to actual persons, either living or dead, is strictly confidential. Every effort has been made to accurately present the views expressed by quotes, stories, or tips herein. The publisher and editors regret any unintentional inaccuracies or omissions, and do not assume responsibility for the opinions herein.

Cover: Kaiyla Barber
Editor: Stephanie Diaz at www.stephaniediazbooks.com

Ordering Information: Impact Learning Publications books are available at special discounts when pruchased in bulk for premiums. Excerpts and custom editions can be created for specific uses. For more information, please email sales@ilpublications.com.
Grown & Gone. — 1st ed.

The publisher is not responsible for websites, profiles, or usernames listed in this book.

Library of Congress Control Number: 2017945594
ISBN: 978-0-9991022-4-4
ISBN: (e-book) 978-0-9991022-9-9

Printed in U.S.A.

0 9 8 7 6 5 4 3 2 1

Table of Contents

introduction

Welcome to *Grown & Gone: Stories and Tips to Help You Survive Your First Independent Year of College*, written by none other than college students. Oh yeah, and one high school senior. We wrote this book to share our stories, experiences, and tips to help you survive freshman year with as few scrapes and bruises as you can. The first year of college can be pretty tough, especially because you really don't know what to expect.

This topic is very important, so I'll ask you to do something for me. Get real comfy before reading this book. Slippers, jammies, sprawling out on the couch (or a cactus plant), whatever defines comfy for you. Some of the contributors of this book have agreed to be transparent and to tell their story as raw as it is, in hopes that they can save you from making some of the mistakes that they made along the way. Others have thought long and hard about what they wanted to share and have given you some straight to the point tips.

This book is about helping you begin your college experience with as much ease as possible. You see, just like you, we all had some ideas about what our freshman year would be, but many of us found out early on that we were wrong. I've added a bit of my experience as well, even though it's been a few years (okay, well maybe more than a few) since I've graduated.

Here's the deal, we all thought we knew what our first year would look like; we had it all planned out -- other than dealing with registration and schedules, which is just as annoying every semester as we thought it would be. The first year of independence can be difficult to navigate. Now don't get me wrong, college is not bad. It's a great experience! But, it's a learning experience. That point will echo itself in many of the stories you read here.

Your first year of college is an introduction to an entirely new world. No more mom and dad to make you study, no teachers asking about your homework, and no one to check up on your grades and reprimand you if you don't do well. Instead, it's all on you. You have to make yourself get up to go to class in the morning, evening, or night, whenever class is scheduled. If you don't turn in your homework—it's a zero.

In most cases, your professor isn't going to follow up with you and ask you where your assignment is. You will get a syllabus at the beginning of the course, and it is *do or die* from there. Very rarely will you be asked to show grades or a report card like you were in high school. In fact, even when someone does inquire, it will usually be a simple *how is school going*, to which most students respond with an *okay*. Surprisingly, most people seem to be fine with that answer. What a change!

If you do this right, you can live out your dreams if you want to; you've just got to work for it. If you stay committed, even during the tough times, you will succeed. Just keep going and don't quit.

The stories you will read are real and honest. We all have an opportunity to learn from each other. It is our hope that the tips and information included will start positive conversation and help you feel even more prepared than you are right now. Each story is different and is based on the writer's personal experience. This means that you might read differing opinions, see a variety of topics, and glean from a diverse set of narratives. Don't forget to read the encouragement center near the end of the book. It contains all the comments from many well-wishers, people you don't even know, who want to see you succeed.

So yes, the secret is out. We wrote this book just for you! It's an exciting time! You are going from a teen in your parent's home to being grown and gone— out of the house and off to college. Get ready! The journey is just getting started.

-Tameka Dyon

KEYAIRA CHIPLIN

a true survival story

WHEN YOU THINK ABOUT college, you think of the amazing time you are going to have away from home. No more taking orders from mama or daddy. Nobody to tell you when you can and cannot have friends over to visit. It is the beginning of your independence, and as seniors in high school, we were all ready for that stage to begin. Well, at least some of us were.

Confused, alone, afraid, misunderstood, lost—words that describe how my freshman college experience was. I did not know what to do or what to expect. Well, honestly, for a minute there, I didn't even think college was going to be in my future.

It all starts in high school. High school is the preparation for your college experience. Unfortunately, my senior year was nothing like that. I lost focus. I got so depressed, I didn't even know who I was. My grades started to slip and I could not focus because there was so much pressure on me.

At my high school, we were required to pass a graduation test before we could graduate. Sounds crazy, huh? I felt so much pressure, knowing that after twelve years of school, I might not be able to graduate because of one test. I was so worried and so stressed out that I failed it. I retook it, and I failed it again. I retook it again, and I failed it again! I started to believe there was no way that I would graduate high school because I could not pass this test.

I decided that there was no reason for me to apply for college, so I didn't. I had given up on myself and lost all hope. I'd even convinced myself that I had no interest in even going to college. It was one week before graduation and after four times of taking the graduation test (yes, I said four), I found out that I had finally passed!

 I passed! Wait, instant dilemma! What do I do now? I hadn't applied for any colleges. I should have been excited, but I wasn't. I couldn't be. I had nothing planned for graduation and had not even been accepted into any schools. How did I get here? What was I going to do? After all, I'd earned all A's and B's in high school. I'd thought I was a good student before this test, but now I was down to absolutely nothing!

College was supposed to be the start of something new for me. It was supposed to be an exciting experience. But, I ended up getting accepted into a school that I really didn't like. I had applied there as a last-ditch effort. If I didn't get accepted into anywhere else, I knew I would get in there...and I did. *Sigh.*

My first semester at this college, I did not feel accepted. Instead, I felt cramped and isolated. I was not enjoying my college experience. I was in a place I didn't want to be. It wasn't fun, but I still tried to do my best in all my classes.

I fought hard that semester and made straight A's! Now that was the best feeling ever! Until it wasn't. That high did not last very long, because I started to get homesick. Yes, I was an 18-year-old who originally couldn't wait to get out of my parent's house, and now all I could think about was going back home. So, I did the unthinkable: I packed up all my stuff, and I moved back home.

 I did not drop out of school; I commuted. Eventually, my grades dropped. I lost focus again, and there were times when I even stopped going to class. I prayed and I prayed, continuously asking God to help me get my head together. Why couldn't I focus? No matter how hard I tried, I ended up in the same funk.

After barely making it in junior college, I tried to get enrolled into a university. Ha! What was I thinking? When the university got my transcripts, they told me that my grades were so horrible that many of the courses could not be transferred. I was literally going to have to start all over.

I thought to myself, *God, when I asked you to help me, I didn't mean like this.* Little did I know, God was answering my prayers all along. He was blessing me with a fresh start. Today, I'm doing well at a university I love. I'm a Dean's Scholar and I founded a non-profit to help teens who may find themselves in the position I was in. I thank God every day for where he brought me.

College is about finding yourself and learning who you are as a person. In college, you develop friendships, figure out your short and long term goals, and find a sense of independency. No one ever said it was going to be easy and I'm not sure why I expected it to be. I wanted to share my story to help high school students, freshmen, or anyone else to understand that when you go to college you are not automatically going to be on the dean's or president's list, you are not necessarily going to make a bunch of new friends, and you surely won't have it all figured out on day one.

I've learned that it's a combination of several things that will help us all be better college students.

Here are some tips that I've gathered along my journey.

- **Use every day as a stepping stool for tomorrow. The knowledge you learn today will help you move closer to your goals of tomorrow.**
- **No matter what your college experience throws at you, stay focused.**
- **Always have a plan. Don't wing it.**
- **Partying is fun, but remember that you have priorities.**
- **Socializing is an amazing part of college and it helps you to begin building a network of friends. If you want to meet people that you have a lot in common with, join clubs. People say you meet your lifetime friends in college.**

It might be difficult at first, but you will slowly figure out how to navigate through college. No matter what happens, don't forget the reason you attended college. Stay true to getting your education, and focus on becoming the best you that you can be. With God on your side, anything is possible.

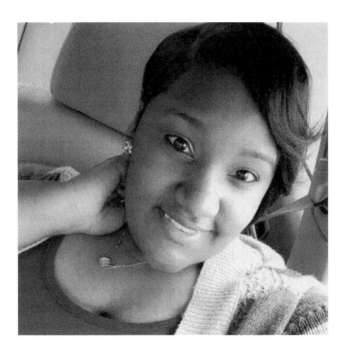

Keyaira Chiplin is 21 and a college student at Alcorn State University. She is currently studying Clinical Psychology and Elementary Education. Keyaira is the Vice President of a women's empowerment organization, Power of Women Expecting Results (POWER). Keyaira is also the founder of an organization she started in Vicksburg, MS. for young teens to help build sisterhood and unity throughout their community called BEAUTY (Beautifying, Educating and Uniting the Youth). She is passionate about motivating others. She says, "God didn't give up on us, so neither should we! Believe in yourself, put your trust in God, and it will all work out in your favor." You can friend her on Facebook at Keyaira Chiplin— to network or to collaborate on any events dealing with motivating the youth or becoming a young entrepreneur.

KYLE KIDD

a solid foundation

WHEN WE FAIL TO lay a solid foundation, we forfeit the opportunity to build a better version of ourselves. At 17, I was blessed with the opportunity to graduate high school one year early, which in turn expedited my transition from adolescence to adulthood. Graduating early meant that I would be entering college a year early. I wasn't concerned because I knew I would have everything under control.

Starting freshman year, I immediately found myself constantly engulfed in the battle between social life and academics. I missed classes without batting an eye. I wanted to be with my friends rather than study for exams. We partied all night without giving any regard to the classes we had the next day.

Of course, these actions affected my grades and my scholarships. By the time spring semester arrived, I realized that I had dug a deep academic hole for myself, so deep that I wanted to quit.

 The problem was that I was not focused on laying a solid foundation for myself. I needed to change my mindset so that I could stand

as an adult and create the foundation necessary for growth during my college years. A positive and focused mindset is your greatest asset as you matriculate through your undergraduate years.

I believe that having the proper mindset and focus will help you to gather new information, which can lead to new ideals and to a successful life. You cannot enter college with the same mindset that you had in high school. Changing your mindset is necessary to ensure that you focus on the tasks assigned to you during your college years.

As a freshman, think about where you want to see yourself by your senior year of college. With an internship? Working in your career? Doing research in your area of study? Entry level position after graduation? All this will come once you push through what I call the Freshman Freedom.

Many of us have experienced the Freshman Freedom at some point. If you haven't, I'm glad you are taking note before you experience it. Freshman Freedom is that feeling you get when you realize you get to be away from home and in control of your actions. You are now an adult. Freshmen become so excited about entering adulthood without realizing that very fact: you are an adult. As an adult, you will be treated like any other person, and unlike your parents, the world shows no mercy to young adults when they make mistakes.

If you want to go to that party tonight but your assignment is due at midnight, sacrifice more time earlier in your day to complete it. Then, you will be able to go out later that night. It's all about prioritizing based on the level of importance. By no means am I saying don't have fun; however, be mindful that there should be a balance between fun and responsibility.

Before you arrive at campus, make a list of three values that you will hold yourself accountable for in the following areas: Academics, Social, and Extracurricular. Once you have figured those out, with every fiber in your body, force yourself to adhere to those values, regardless of the situation.

Your freshman year is a pivotal moment that can determine the success of your undergraduate years. Once you enter your collegiate career, what will your goals as a freshman be? There needs to be a plan in place. Set your expectations: What GPA do you want? How many organizations do you want to join? How many hours of study will you need to dedicate to classes daily? The power is now in your hands. If you balance it wisely, you will gain control of all four years of your college experience. This is all a part of laying your foundation.

My grandmother once told me that I didn't know what it was like to be hungry. As a child, I thought this was an absurd thing to say, considering that I ate all the time! But, she didn't mean it in a literal sense. What she meant was that I didn't know what it was like to want something intensely, to have a hunger for your passion that caused you to work day and night until you got it. As college students, we often have this mindset that doors will automatically open for us, and opportunities will fall in our laps. Sadly, we are mistaken.

In the world we live in, you must be proactive in your pursuit to success. In college, no opportunity is given to you. It must all be earned through work in the classroom, research in your area of study, and constant work throughout campus. There aren't many internships offered to freshmen in college; however, that shouldn't stop you from doing research into internships and preparing yourself. Consider looking into scholarships, internships, and graduate schools of your choice so that you build your foundation early of what you want to do later in your collegiate career.

 After my initial experience, I decided to start anew. I transferred to another school. Currently, I am a senior at Jackson State University. Upon my arrival, I was dedicated. I committed to myself that I would put my best foot forward and become involved in campus activities. I knew that I did not

want to be a regular student. Instead, I decided to be a change agent, building a positive campus experience for students.

In life, we have people who are leading and making a change; then, we have those who are on the sidelines watching the change come about. You must choose for yourself, do you want to watch or do you want to work?

Every April at our school is election season. Election season is when many students pursue big positions on campus to run for and get elected into the next academic year. I was not able to join the election season; however, I had the opportunity to fill a vacant position as VP of Programming for the Campus Activities Board. The Campus Activities Board is a very prominent organization whose job is to host and implement all campus educational and entertainment events for the students.

At first, I was hesitant about applying because I did not know anybody; however, what I did know was that I had the right skills for the position. I applied and landed an interview. Because I took that bold step towards success, I got the position. I served as Vice President for one year and I was recently elected to serve as President of the Campus Activities Board for my senior year. This all happened in one year!

As a Mass Communications major, I have become the first student at Jackson State to write for the #1 HBCU publication in the country, HBCUBuzz. Would you believe it if I told you I had little experience in journalism prior to this? I applied for the position with only an essay I did in class and my resume.

Since then, I have become a Sports Editor for Black Beat Sports, CampusLATELY Author, and have written some HBCUBuzz's top stories. Success looks for no one! I went out and looked for it! Sometimes success is waiting for you in a certain place in your life, but you won't know it unless you make the decisions and the moves to get to that place. Are you willing to go there? Are you willing to take the initiative for something that you want?

I have been able to travel the country as a Student Leader and I have received scholarships for the time and effort put into my job. In your own life, what is it that you want to do? Who do you want to impact? Why can't you do that right now?

What is holding you back from achieving that goal today? Ask yourself these questions, and then begin to do the work necessary for success.

As young adults and Millennials, we can sometimes have a sense of entitlement. Some of us believe that the things we receive should be served to us on a golden platter and we shouldn't have to exert too much energy to get it. In the real world, that way of thinking is the easiest way to miss out on great opportunities. To succeed you will need to dedicate your time, effort, work, and willpower. You must be willing to go beyond what you are comfortable with to receive something different from what you have been getting. I wish you great success in your journey!

Kyle Kidd-Buckner, a 20-year-old senior, is a Mass
Communication major with emphasis in Multimedia
Journalism at Jackson State University. He served as Vice
President of Programming for the Campus Activities Board
for the 2016-2017 year and as a Staff Writer for Jackson
State's school newspaper, "The Blue & White Flash."
He was recently appointed to the position of Executive
President for the Campus Activities Board for the 2017-2018
academic school year. He serves as an Author for HBCUBuzz
and Collegiate Sports Editor of Black Beat Sports. Recently
was appointed as Contributor of DoerHouse, LLC. He was the
2016 National Conference on Student Leadership scholarship
recipient, being the first HBCU student to be awarded. Kyle
looks to one day publish his own book, become an
Entertainment and Political reporter, as well as an Executive
Producer. Follow Kyle on Instagram @iamkylekidd, Twitter
@kyled_kidd, and Facebook @KyleDewayneKidd.

A'MYA JONES

don't wait, activate!

IF THERE IS ANYTHING that college has taught me, it is to value every moment of my time and use it wisely. While in college, you are going to encounter a lot of tedious assignments. These assignments may not always be difficult, but they will be time consuming. This work will take up most, if not all, of your time. It can be very overwhelming. After all, you are in a totally different environment and you are excited. You are in college surrounded by lots of interesting people on a daily basis. Who wants to be in their dorm doing homework all day when there is so much to experience? Because of that, you must prioritize your time. If there were ever a piece of advice I wish someone had given me, it would've been to DWA: Don't Wait, Activate.

What I mean by DWA is, once your professor gives you an assignment, don't hesitate to begin on it. This doesn't mean that you must finish the assignment the first day you receive it. What I am suggesting is that you at least acknowledge it.

For example, if it is a research paper, go ahead and look for some great sources to use. You don't have to begin research the same day, but by finding the sources the same day, you'll have trained your brain to do a little a day until the assignment is finished.

This activating method can also be used when studying for certain subjects and exams. Study habits that help you stray from procrastination are quite helpful and will prepare you for your journey away from high school and into college life.

Procrastination is a common problem for first-year college students and none of us ever think that we will be affected by it. We truly believe that we have everything under control. It's in that final moment that we realize we've ended up waiting until the last minute to get what we needed done.

I thought the same thing. I graduated from high school with honors and I was even the student body president of my graduating class. I never, not in a million years, believed that I would fall into a pattern of procrastination. But I did, and it was easy. I fell into the trap very quickly.

What I had to realize is that college is not high school. If you don't approach it with your game face on from day one, you may not be happy with your performance. So, remember to activate your inner go getter. Don't let procrastination get you.

College is a lot of fun! There are so many organizations you can become a part of, so many people, places, and things you will encounter. It's a never-ending cycle of discovery and enlightenment. That's why I'm advising you to start practicing these habits early so you can enjoy the full experience guilt-free and not constantly be afraid to check your GPA.

Try to stay ahead in all your classes. This will give you room and time to fit in any extracurricular activities you would like to do, whether that is catching a movie with friends, eating out, hanging at the mall, or going to the biggest party of the semester.

You feel good when you know you have everything under control, when you know you have your priorities in order. Take your college experience seriously—it determines what you do with the rest of your life...or not. Instead, you could wait until the last minute to complete your assignments, be tired all the time from staying up late once you get behind, and not get the grades you were aiming for.

 Always keep in mind that procrastination leads to devastation so remember to DWA: Don't Wait, Activate!

A'Mya Jones is a recent graduate of the MS School of the Arts where she served as student body president with a focus in Theatre. She is currently enrolled at the University of Mississippi with a double major, obtaining a B.A. in Theatre arts and a degree in Liberal Studies emphasizing in English, Spanish, and African American Studies. Upon graduation, A'mya plans to attend Harvard Law School and obtain her doctorate in entertainment law. Her favorite quote is: "Never let the fear of striking out, keep you from playing the game." Follow her on Facebook @a'myajones, Instagram @tha_myaj_way & amya.jones_, and Snapchat @MyaJ34

MARKIE'SHA JAMES

the complete college experience

AS A COLLEGE STUDENT, you will find yourself struggling emotionally, financially, spiritually, or even all three at once. While in high school, I was involved in everything—you can almost take that literally. I was Miss Murrah, Student Body Representative, in almost every organization that the school had to offer, and band. Coming to college I was expecting to be just as social. Boy, was I in for a rude awakening. I came to college with a lot of people that I knew, but I did not look at my *new beginning* in a positive way. I remember thinking, *ughh, I have to start all the way over!* Going to college is a new beginning, but in a good way. All the things that you learned before college and everything you learn while in college, whether good or bad, should be used in a way to better you as a person.

I have lived on campus every year. At first, I was constantly telling my mom, *I'm stayin' at home. I don't want to live on campus.* My mom was not having that, and she encouraged me to stay on campus to have what she considered the complete college experience. Looking back on it, I appreciate it because I could further develop a sense of independence and identity.

My first roommate was one of my best friends from high school and everything went well until we just got tired of being around each other all the time. We respected each other's items and space. However, I have heard many stories where people have roomed with their close friends and it did not go well. I would suggest when choosing a roommate, choose someone that you are not around all the time. This choice will help you get to know other people.

 When it comes to dorm life, it is important that you know what type of environment you would like to live in. Don't be afraid to get to know new people. If you have a roommate, be sure to establish boundaries and responsibilities shortly after moving in. This will eliminate issues that may come up in the future.

The best advice that anyone could have given me is that college is not perfect, and you must enjoy your years socially and academically. Don't be afraid to ask questions. It's true what they say, *a closed mouth never gets fed!*

Markie'Sha James was born in Itta Benna, MS. In 2001, she moved to Jackson, Mississippi. This move was important because she struggled with severe asthma and the nearest treatment place was in Jackson. Markie'Sha is a product of Jackson Public Schools. She was named Miss. Murrah at William B. Murrah High School. Currently, she attends Jackson State University, majoring in honors chemistry. She is the president of the American Chemical Society and a member of the Partnership for Research and Education in Materials. In 2016 Markie'Sha was recognized as one of the five L'Oréal and Tom Joyner "Young Women with a Purpose" scholarship recipients and a Who's Who Among Students in American Colleges and Universities. While attending university, Markei'Sha had the opportunity of exploring research at Jackson State University, University of Mississippi Medical Center, and L'Oreal USA. She aspires to have a career that allows her to combine her life experiences with her love for science, with a goal of improving the quality of life for all.

CHARDE LYONS

talk to someone

WHEN I WENT TO college, I was excited. I knew that I would have everything under control, after all, I was grown. I was determined to have the best college experience ever! To my surprise, I did the total opposite. I did everything in that first year completely wrong; I did not take anyone's advice. I jumped into a toxic relationship with a guy. I strayed away from school. Because of those choices, I got behind. I stopped reading the Bible, going to church, and trying to strengthen my relationship with God.

Everything that I was doing well when I was in high school somehow seemed to be a struggle now. The man that I thought loved me, my boyfriend, was physically and mentally abusive. I became depressed and had severe anxiety.

Now, I wasn't going to tell anybody my business. I didn't share with anyone what I was going through. Over time, the situation got worse. I didn't know what to do so I began to isolate myself. My family constantly asked me if anything was wrong. Instead of being honest with them, I would disappear for days at a time. I guess you can say, I lost my mind.

Honestly, at the time, I was not aware of this. I knew I was going through some things, but I really couldn't see the severity of my actions. By the end

of my freshman year, I had pushed everyone away.
I felt as though I had nowhere to turn. I had no one
to talk to, not even this guy who was supposed be
my boyfriend. To make matters worse, my
relationship with God was going downhill.

I'm glad that I came to my senses, but that
was not without its fair share of hardships. I'd laid
out a rocky path for myself and now I had no
choice but to see things through. I was determined
to fix every aspect of my life, one mistake at a time.

I finally realized I needed God more than
anything. I needed Him to lead me and guide me
through school. I learned a lot that year. Probably
because I made every mistake you could ever think
of. Here are a few things I learned during my
freshman year.

First, don't rush anything – That goes for
relationships and school. Take your time; you are
young. Let your focus be school: homework, tests,

and studying. If you are in an abusive relationship, get away or seek help as soon as possible.

Second, don't stray away from God – Whatever your religion may be, don't let anyone or anything keep you from it. If you need help, here is one of my favorite scriptures: Philippians 4:13 – I can do all things through Christ which strengthens me.

Third, stay in contact with your family – At the end of the day, your family will be all you have, whether you want them to or not. Also, life is short. You must stay in touch.

Fourth, get involved – Get out of your dorm! Meet new people! Believe it or not, there is so much you can do on campus. You will be amazed at all the events and extracurricular activities you can participate in.

Fifth, talk to someone – Don't be afraid. If you are feeling depressed, anxious, even suicidal, please, I'm begging you, talk to someone. There is always someone that you can talk to; whether its family, friends, or the counselors at your school.

My final tip is to have fun! Trying to do good in college does not mean you cannot have fun.

Enjoy your college experience. It is possible to do good in school and enjoy yourself.

 If you are wondering if I ever got to redo my college experience, I did. One thing I can say is, it is never too late. I eventually graduated with my Associates degree and now I attend Mississippi State University studying Kinesiology. I got out of that toxic relationship. I met someone new and things are progressing nicely. My relationship with God is getting stronger and stronger as the days go on. I am finally happy and I couldn't be any happier. God Bless!

Charde Lyons is currently a Junior at Mississippi State University, pursuing a Bachelor's degree in Kinesiology. She previously obtained her Associates of Arts degree from Hinds Community College. Charde enjoys reading books, hanging with friends, and watching movies. Follow Charde on Facebook and Snapchat at @charde.denise.

ELIZABETH GONZALEZ

high school transition

TRANSITIONING FROM HIGH SCHOOL to college did not occur as I had originally planned. I graduated high school believing that I would be attending my dream four-year university. Instead, I ended up settling for the education provided at a local community college, minus a functioning car.

I learned early on that change is inevitable and does not necessarily have to be a bad thing. So yes, I had to settle for an alternative route than I had originally planned, but I was lucky enough to have a backup plan. At the time, the following questions riveted me: Is college hard? How intense are the lectures? Labs? Are the classes big? Is the food good? What of the social environment? Now knowing everything that I do, my answers to the above-mentioned questions are quite simple. It depends on your university of choice.

One answer is certain to me: college is hard. I say this not to intimidate you, but to congratulate you for choosing to embark on this journey, for it is no easy feat. Prepare to study—and study long and hard.

 Pay attention in your lecture classes and try your hardest to attend class. Yes, being in college means being in school for less hours and frequency, but try to go to class and take good notes. This does not literally mean that you will write

down every word that your instructor says, but try to challenge your thinking.

Come to class prepared. Look over your assigned reading material the previous night. You do not necessarily have to read the hundreds of pages that were assigned to you, but skim over the text. Look at the objectives highlighted at the beginning of the chapters and review the key points stated at the end of the chapter. Make sure to create a list of questions and strive to answer these questions in class.

It is important for you to speak up in class! You do not understand how vital this fact is to your overall collegiate experience! Make it a personal mission to introduce yourself to your instructor on the first day of class and forward any questions— whether that may be in person or through email— promptly. Not only are you informing your instructor of your devotedness to your academic grades, but use these professors for the resources that they are!

I highly vouch for you to establish these connections, for in the long run they can be used for references, future jobs, future opportunities, etc. I can personally advocate for this fact; I am currently working as a Research Assistant for a cancer study at a local community clinic. I would not have known of this opportunity if I had not spoken to my instructor and expressed my interest in specializing in oncology (she happens to be the head instructor of the oncology program at my university---I know, gasp!).

I also recommend you spice up your seating selections. I have personally noted (I, too, have suffered of this common phenomenon) that we, college students, tend to stick to the same seating arrangement that we selected on the very first day of class. I urge you to be bold! Socialize. College is not like high school. You will not frequently see the same people in your pre-requisite courses (unless they are in your major and/or minor) and that is not taking into account the number of students in your classroom. Trust me, I have been there!

I took a pathophysiology course with more than one-hundred people in my class. Socializing can be scary and this fear often inspires us to detach ourselves from everyone around us. Break this vicious cycle. Sit where you learn best and socialize without getting too distracted.

I encourage you to get familiar with your learning style to help simplify this decision. Learn whether you are a visual, aural, verbal, physical, or logical learner. Embrace these unique characteristics, they are your strengths.

I also highly encourage you to test your limits. Learn how much you can handle at once. I learned quickly that I could not be a full-time student working two jobs and enrolled in five different student organizations. My grades suffered slightly as a result, so please learn from my mistakes! If you are lucky enough to find a flexible job that meets your needs, then good for you!

Nonetheless, your first and most important job is being a good student. Yes, it sounds cheesy, but believe me when I say that your grades matter! Your GPA matters. For many of us, scholarships depend on maintaining a high GPA. Take this role seriously.

Make a habit of setting deadlines for yourself. I advocate for creating a to-do list. It does not have to be daily per se, but own one. Have it with you always. What worked best for me was synchronizing my monthly calendar with due dates to my phone. I would get alerts when an approaching deadline neared and kept my procrastination at bay.

If you do not own a google account, create one. It was a huge relief to back-up my data on Google drive. Additionally, I encourage you to have other back-ups to your back-up (e.g. flash-drives, hard-drives, email, etc.). You cannot believe the distress I once suffered when I misplaced a hard-drive containing the essay that I had stressed over for a whole week. Needless to say, I haven't suffered with this issue again.

Furthermore, when you need help, get help. Sounds simple enough, but sometimes our pride tends to get a little bruised at the prospect of asking others for help. Again, I bring up the resources card.

This past semester I had the misfortune of having a family member placed on hospice services. The impact it had on me psychologically, physically, and emotionally is not something that I wish upon any student. The toll it had on me was great; however, what aided me was relaying to the available departments of my school this vital information. I worked with Student Life and the Counseling Center, which positively influenced my situation.

If life happens to you, know you are not alone. The faculty and staff at your school are deeply invested in you and never be afraid to befriend them. I was fortunate enough to have met several faculty members that, with time, have become great mentors and friends to me. I wish for every student out there to have a similar experience.

Lastly, I want to drill into your head to have fun! I know that it can be hard at times with deadlines occurring simultaneously, but seriously, don't forget to treat yourself. Make sure to schedule some time for yourself to go to the movies, hang out with friends, and just relax. Balance is vital to your overall success. Be kind to yourself. Make sure to reward yourself even if you didn't do too well on the test that you stayed up the whole night studying for. You are trying. That is what matters!

 This includes establishing a solid sleep and eating schedule. It is so easy to become overwhelmed by the tasks at hand that we forget our basic necessities. Always carry snacks with you to class, stay hydrated, and catch some zzzz's. Maybe that is just the inner nurse in me speaking, but you cannot perform at your optimal level without the proper fuel. Best of luck to you in the future. Dream big and

never give up—especially when things get hard. You are a capable individual.

 It is important for you to speak up in class! You do not understand how vital this fact is to your overall collegiate experience!!

Elizabeth Gonzalez is a nursing major and fine-arts minor at Texas Christian University (TCU). She is expected to graduate with her Bachelors of Science in Nursing on December 2018. Before attending TCU, Elizabeth attended Tarrant County College where she received her Associates of Arts and Texas Woman's University before transferring. She has been involved in countless student organizations, such as Phi Theta Kapa (Role: VP of Fellowship), the Student Government Association (Roles: Vice-President, Parliamentarian, and Senate Chair), and the Student Nurses Association (Role: Treasurer) to name a few. Like most college students, Elizabeth's biggest obstacle is her procrastination (which is a work in progress). She loves to study at the TCU Library. She enjoys caring for her cat, Ferocious, long runs, painting, reading, and shopping. Elizabeth is also a first-generation student in her family and seeks to use her bilingual skills in her role as an oncology nurse and future art therapist. Follow Elizabeth on Facebook at @elizabethgonzalez.

XAVIER SMITH

no advantage over me or my life

THIS IS FOR MY SISTERS. I think that many of us go through similar situations, so I wanted to share with you how I got distracted in my first year of college.

When a man says, *I like you* or *I want to be with you forever*, it's not always true. But something about being in college, on my own, made me feel grown. Like I knew the best thing to do in almost every situation, like I had control over my life, and like I was in love for the very first time.

My freshman year at Tougaloo I did the exact opposite of what I'm about to tell you. I believed a guy who said, *I like you*. All the things my mom had taught me went out the window. This one guy ran the worst game on me.

Even worse, it nearly killed me inside when I found out that he was not the good guy I thought he was. My grades dropped, I missed classes, and I just really didn't care about school. Then, I found out he was dating a girl I thought was my friend. *Could things get any worse?*

You see, freshman year can make or break you. Not to say that you will have this same problem, but boys can really make you lose focus and lose sight of what you came to college for in the first place, your education. There can be harsh consequences when you do things without thinking them through. Losing focus could determine whether you graduate on time, or stay in college for five, six, or even seven years. Losing focus can also make you consider dropping out.

In my case, because of my lack of focus, freshman year broke me, and when I say broke me, it broke me all the way down. My first time living away from home, I was foot loose and fancy free, doing my own thing. Well, except for washing my clothes, my mom took care of that.

I would never go to my early morning classes because the night before I wouldn't leave the boys' dorm until almost two or three in the morning, drinking, smoking weed, doing all the wrong things. My friends and I loved to room hop, you know, go from one guy's room to the next. Well, after months of partying, it finally caught up to me.

 Sex + no protection = pregnant. Now, that is basic math that you do not want to learn. He said he wanted to be in a relationship with me and I believed him. Now, I had to go and tell my mom that I am pregnant. I was 18 years old, a freshman, with no job. I had nowhere for a baby to live. I had no clue of what I was going to do, but at least I had him… or so I thought.

After finding out that this boy did not want me and that he was seeing my best friend, I fell into depression. I thought I was going to have to quit school. I didn't know what to do. How would I live? Shoot, where would I live?

Luckily, my mom supported me. She has always been there for me. She helped me to regain my focus and turn things around. I didn't have to quit school. Today, my grades are good. I have great mentors in many of my professors. And best of all, I'm about to graduate from Tougaloo College.

I look back on the mistakes I made, and I thank God, because there are many girls who were making the same mistakes I was. They were focused on some guy and got pregnant. Some girls have no choice but to quit and find themselves working at a low wage job trying to take care of their child(ren).

I jumped at the opportunity to be a part of this project. Maybe someone else would be embarrassed by their story but I'm not. I'm not happy about the choices I made, but I'm happy about the outcome. I hope that my story can help someone else to avoid making the same mistakes that I made. If I could give any advice it would be these three things.

First, don't lose sight of the reason why you attended college. I was in church for most of my life, and when I got a little bit of freedom and could make my own decisions, I went buck wild. I did all the things I saw other people doing in high school that I could never do. I thought those things were fun, but they only got me in a world of trouble. My mom really tried to raise me right, but I lost sight of all of that for a minute.

 You have expectations of yourself and that's why you are attending college. You want to build a better life for yourself, not make it worse. Focus on your future, take your college life and your grades seriously. Every decision that you make in college could follow you for the rest of your life, so think carefully and make good ones. That's not to say that you won't ever make mistakes, but if you are confused about something, get advice from your parents. Yes, you are grown, but everyone needs a little help every now and then.

Second, get rid of all distractions. Focus on yourself and learning more about who you are as a person. This is your first time being out on your own, so you've never had to make a lot of the decisions you will have to make now while you are in college. You don't need distractions. Especially if they are negative distractions that will keep you away from class, keep you in a lot of drama, or prevent you from doing your work.

Did you know your friends can be distractions too? Trying to get you to go to parties, distracting you from getting the assignment due tomorrow completed, and convincing you that you can do it later are all forms of distractions. Peer pressure can be difficult to overcome. But, if you stay focused and refuse to allow them to distract you from what you really should be doing, you will do fine.

Third, when you make a mistake—and you will, because no one is perfect—don't beat yourself up to the point of where you can't stand up, own up, fix it, and be a better you. Learn from your mistakes and move on from them. Do everything you can to make each day better than the previous day.

I hope my story will encourage you to stay focused. No one has control over you or your life but *YOU*. It's your decisions that make you great or not. Which do you want to be? I know I want to be great and since freshman year, I've strived to do just that.

Although this work was written while Xavier Smith was in college, she is now a graduate of Tougaloo College. She received a Bachelor of Arts in Mass Communications on May 7, 2017. Xavier lives in Jackson, MS and is a product of the Jackson public school system. Xavier is the owner of XAS Photography. Photography and videography are her passion. She aspires to be a producer. Xavier is on the Praise and Worship Team at her church. She loves the Lord and her family. Follow XAS Photography on Facebook @xasphotography.

MERCEDES ALLEN

cultivate your passion

DON'T BE AFRAID to get out of your comfort zone. If you are afraid of trying something new, then you are afraid to grow into the person you are destined to be. Now is the time to explore and try out new things. You do not want to look back on your college years and regret not taking any chances.

The quicker you try new things, the more you'll know what your likes and dislikes are. Trying new things will help you after you graduate and prevent you from being indecisive.

College is a part of your discovery years. My freshman year, I worked in the biomedical engineering part of campus helping with research. I enjoyed learning about the projects, but not the scientific equation side.

I also took an Earth Science class, and even thought about being a dietician. But, I was led back to my gut of being in business, and pursued my marketing degree.

Find out what your passion is and do not wait another second to pursue it.

Having a goal in mind kept me focused and made going to class enjoyable. I got to do the groundwork for my start-up and even participate in competitions to get funding from investors. I was not thinking about changing my major to something I thought would make more money.

Focusing too much on the money that a given field will deliver will cause you to be miserable and lose motivation. You should give yourself time to decide what you like and then pursue that degree. If you want to be an accountant, learn and get excited about the coursework.

Find out what your passion is, and do not wait another second to pursue it. By the time you graduate not only will you have experience, but an extra boost as to why you get up every day to do the work you love.

 I enjoyed college a lot because I was really involved. In addition to interning, I was a Resident Advisor and an international conversation partner. As a conversation partner, I would be paired with an international student each semester, where we shared cultural backgrounds and interests to make campus adjustments easier. I got

to meet a Turkish grad student who caught on quickly to learning English, and a guy from Korea who killed in ping pong—these are moments I still remember.

Change majors, take advantage of campus programs, and learn about people who look different than you. This is the perfect opportunity to meet people from various countries and learn that the world is bigger than your hometown. There is no exaggerating—if done right, your college years will be some of the best years of your life. Enjoy!

Mercedes Allen is from Jackson, MS, and a Marketing graduate of Mississippi State University. Currently residing in Dallas, TX, Mercedes is a Digital Marketing Consultant. When she is not creating digital media solutions for companies, blogging, or managing projects, Mercedes is working on her college start-up. The mobile application, Campus Resell, is set to be available for downloading in 2017. Connect with Mercedes at letscreateit@sadiedailymedia.com, @sadiedailymedia on social media, or www.sadiedailymedia.com.

JASMINE WHIPPS

seek God for yourself

I REMEMBER MOVING IN my freshman year. I was slightly afraid, very shy, but also very excited. I was grateful to have my best friend living down the hall from me and a few other friends attending the college as well in the same major. My parents told me a thousand times to be mindful of who I was around, to watch my surroundings, and not to walk around at night by myself.

I received an entire pep talk, even after spending my junior and senior year at a residential high school. Being the careful person I am, I pretty much kept with what they told me. But what did they know about college life anyway?

I was ready to live and enjoy life. And I did! I enjoyed the campus life even more than high school. I thought campus life equalled more freedom. But what I didn't realize at the time was that with more freedom comes greater responsibility.

If you're reading this, I'm sure you've probably heard the same speech I was given a hundred times by now, so I won't make it one hundred and one, but allow me to share a bit of advice.

 If you're anything like me, you've probably grown up in church. It's the place I knew I would be every Sunday morning and every Wednesday evening, no matter what. By no matter

what, I mean rain, snow, sleet, or shine, we were there. Don't abandon that!

The greatest lesson I learned was to truly seek God for myself. Ironically, I accepted my calling into ministry my first year of college. Trust me when I say that He is truly the one to depend on during this time. Things will get hard in college, but trusting Him will make it all better, even if it doesn't seem like it. He truly moves mountains.

Another thing I learned along the way was to never compromise my moral beliefs. Peer pressure is real, and if you thought high school was something, then you are in for a surprise because college is a different level. It doesn't get better; the peer pressure gets worse. Don't compromise who you are to fit in!

If your gut (or the Holy Spirit) is telling you don't do it, then do not do it! It's not worth it in the end. If people can't accept that, you don't need them in your life. Never let someone disrespect who you are, especially if it's not adding to your growth.

Everything is new. You might be coming from a different environment than where you go to college, so expect change. Don't expect things to be the same and as cliché as it sounds, expect the unexpected. Don't be afraid to grow and experience new situations. It's all part of the journey.

Stay you! You're beautiful/handsome, inside and out! Keep being who you are regardless of what goes on. Those who are meant to be part of the journey will accept you for exactly who you are. Have fun! You don't have to stay stuck in your dorm room and you don't have to be a party hopper to have fun in college. Find a happy medium. You're going to make it!! Relax and smile! Enjoy your freshman year!

Don't expect things to be the same and as cliché as it sounds, expect the unexpected.

Jasmine Whipps is 22 years old and attends Tougaloo College. She is set to graduate in 2018 with a B.A. in Music Education. Jasmine is a Social Media Consultant and Graphic Designer. She is also a worship leader at Greater Peace International Ministries. Follow Jasmine on Twitter @_PoeticQueen, Facebook @JasmineNicoleWhipps, and Instagram @poeticqueenjaz.

10

ADESUWA EKUNWE

no one likes a perfect story

MY SENIOR YEAR OF high school started out like a dream. My friendships were stronger than ever. I was voted into the student council, nominated for Arrow Court and class favorite, and I got a scholarship to my dream school. I was on cloud nine, but that high was about to be short-lived.

One morning, what I believed to be a normal day was nothing close to normal. My parents had been acting weird all week and on this day they sat me down to talk. They told me that my father had a doctor's appointment and they had found cancer in his stomach. They said that he was going to have surgery to remove the cancer, but it would also remove a portion of his stomach.

I was scared out of my mind. Surgery was never easy, and it was scheduled to take place two months before my high school graduation. I wanted to be a doctor, and I knew that surgery came with risks, but it was the only option.

The day of the surgery was gruesome. The atmosphere was filled with anxiety, but luckily my father's cancer was removed. Afterwards, the doctors explained that he would have to go through chemotherapy and radiation. Although it was a long journey, two months later, I graduated from high school with my father watching from the stands.

I decided to attend Jackson State University to be closer to my family for obvious reasons. To be quite honest, I was disappointed that I wasn't moving on to the place where I wanted to be, but I knew I was in the place that I needed to be.

Entering my first year of college, I was filled with excitement and ambitions. I wanted it to be perfect, especially since my senior year in high school had been so lackluster. I roomed with my best friend and I joined a lot of organizations. I studied hard and finished the first semester with a strong GPA and a prestigious internship at a medical facility to match. Everything that I had planned and hoped for was happening. It was perfect. Little did I know, this was all the calm before the storm.

The following year, my father's cancer had returned in full force. We were told that no amount of surgery, chemotherapy, or radiation was going to save his life. We just had to have faith and take the days one day at a time. The doctors went ahead and scheduled another surgery to remove my father's entire stomach that summer. There were side effects. My father had constant hiccups and he threw up all the time.

That summer, I traveled back and forth to the hospital to watch my dad. My mom and I did our best to make sure that my father was comfortable, but it was hard. I watched the strongest man I knew turn into a skeleton. He could barely walk.

I am not one to complain or talk about my problems, so I went around campus like everything was fine. I pretended that my life was perfect because that was what I was used to. I kept my family life secret, but the effects were visible. I would skip class. I would overeat. Some days I just skipped class to cry. I didn't talk to anyone. All my emotions were bundled up because my perfect world was crumbling around me.

During winter break and four days before Christmas, my father passed away. The battle was lost. I felt like I had lost control. Every aspect of my life was suffering. I gained weight and I failed most of my classes. I was told that I would have to repeat. This was something that I never experienced. I was depressed. I stayed home most of that semester, but nothing helped. I had lost my father, but mostly I had lost my sense of purpose and ambition.

I didn't care about school. I didn't care about anything except for the fact that my father wasn't there. He would never be able to see me graduate college or walk me down the aisle or meet my children.

One day in the library, my classmate approached me. He said that he noticed that my spark was gone. I told him what I was going through, but I mainly talked about how I felt that my goals of medical school were doomed. He looked me in the eyes and said, *no one likes a perfect story Adesuwa.*

He told me to look at all the successful people in history and that the one thing that they had in common was that their paths were never how they'd originally planned. It wasn't perfect.

 It would never be perfect. Successful people were those who didn't let their failures define them. They took those failures and used them as power and motivation. That is what I had to do and that's what I did.

I turned my pitfalls into motivation, and I am here to tell you that there is light at the end of the tunnel. My story may not be the typical freshman tips that you expected, but I wanted what I went through to be a guiding light for you. Go into your freshman year ready to take the bull by the horns. Do not be afraid to fail and don't aim to be perfect. Take this life that you have and live it to the fullest. Take risk and make the most out of each day. Remember, nobody likes a perfect story.

Adesuwa Ekunwe was born in Lansing, Michigan. However, she claims Mississippi as her home. She was raised in Clinton, Mississippi and graduated from Clinton High School. After completing high school, Adesuwa chose to attend Jackson State University, where both of her parents were alumni and faculty. Adesuwa is an honors chemistry pre-medicine major at Jackson State University. She is Vice President of the American Chemical Society and is a student researcher for the Partnership for Research and Education in Materials program. She recently founded the Jackson State University Dance Marathon, which aims to raise funds for the local children's hospital. After completing her duration at Jackson State University, Adesuwa plans to attend medical school with the aim of becoming a surgeon or Pediatric Oncologist. She hopes to devote some of her medical career to aiding underdeveloped countries and eventually train future medical students. Follow Adesuwa at @daisiesxo.

11

JAY LITTLE

turning tides

YOUR COLLEGE CAREER WILL be one of the best experiences of your life. It provides a foundation to who you will become and experiences that will shape the way you see the world. As a small-town guy who has always excelled in academia, I considered myself to be beyond ready for college and even more excited to be moving away from home.

Eager to experience the first breathe of campus air, I applied to multiple colleges and scholarships and ultimately came to a decision to attend the University of Alabama. UA provided a great campus atmosphere that offered a beautiful campus, superb student life, and amazing athletics.

 College was a life changing transition. Originating from the small town of Artesia, Mississippi, I became accustomed to the sense of small community. I attended a small high school where there were only forty-seven students in my graduating class. These demographics made it easy to become a star student at my school and in the community. I had always been a high achiever throughout my academic career and took much pride in my successes. Acquiring numerous leadership positions in organizations on and off campus, it was clear that I was making strides in my community. I graduated at the top of my class as salutatorian and received a countless

number of accolades. I was ready for college and all that it had to offer.

When I officially began my career at Bama, I quickly came to a daunting realization. Who I was at home didn't matter when I got to college. I didn't know anyone and I didn't have friends or connections. In a sense, I didn't matter. It felt like my high school resume had just been tossed into the fiery pit of irrelevance. I wanted to get involved, much like I was in high school, but I didn't know where to turn.

Here's what I learned: College is about new beginnings and poses amazing opportunities to find yourself and discover the depths of your interests and passions. You are no longer a big fish in a small pond; the roles are reversed. You are a small fish in a big pond. You will have to figure out how to navigate this huge and unfamiliar campus. How are you going to define yourself? What do you seek to accomplish and what will your legacy be? How will people remember you after you graduate? These are all questions that I posed after accepting my impending fate. I didn't budge and I set out on my new-found freedom with excitement, eagerness, and goals.

One of the most important things that I have found to be essential to a college career is social life and involvement. College is forty percent academia, and sixty percent everything else. What you do outside of the class shapes your educational career. The people you meet, the organizations you join, and how you impact your college community are pillars of your educational hierarchy. Involvement is crucial to a well-rounded academic experience and you can gain experience through activities, clubs, and organizations.

I urge everyone to find their niche, group, or community. Seemingly, those with similar goals. Some organizations that I joined were Student Government Association, National Society of Black Engineers, Black Student Union, and the Center for Service and Leadership, just to name a few. Not only did these organizations benefit me personally, but also professionally. I truly began to find out who I was as an individual and as a leader.

 There are a few final points of conquering one's collegiate experience. The main and most crucial factor would be to always stay true to yourself. Though I had migrated from home and embarked on a new journey, I never lost sight of who I was, and I didn't let my environment alter my behavior.

Next would be to remember what you have done to get to this point. I may be in an unfamiliar environment, but my prior experiences have made me who I am and I ensured that I continued my legacy of success and excellence.

Remember that your decisions affect more than just you. I realized that I was an active representation of my parents, hometown, and young African-American men. This allowed me to understand that I have a purpose, duty and responsibility. I could not let these people down. I had to act with those people in mind, which leads me to my next point.

Remember to thank those who've helped, believed or invested in you. After I had gotten comfortable with the environment, I once again contacted those who have been influential in my prior academic experience. If it weren't for those people, I'm not sure that I would be the person that I am now, and it is important that I relayed that to them.

The final crucial factor would be to actively give back. Your college community is your home for at least the next four years and it is the responsibility of its citizens to care for it. I volunteer in and around the Tuscaloosa area because I want to better the lives of those around me and truly show that this is my home as well. My decisive point is to simply make it count! These will be the greatest years of your life and you definitely want to enjoy it the fullest.

The University of Alabama has provided me with life changing experiences, great academics, and awesome friends. I urge any upcoming or current college student to harness what your institutions have to offer because this is a once in a lifetime opportunity. You're young, careless, free, and most likely broke. What do you have to lose?

Jay Little is a 2016 Gates Millennium Scholar at the University of Alabama. A native of Artesia, MS, he is studying Computer Science with a minor in Civic Engagement and Leadership. Little is also a member of the STEM Path to MBA Program and University Honors. He is actively involved in the UA community with SGA, where he serves as Assistant Vice President for Student Affairs, National Society of Black Engineers (NSBE) PCI Chairman, Association for Computing Machinery (ACM), Black Student Union (BSU), The Blackburn Institute, Collegiate 100 Black Men and an active volunteer with the Center for Service and Leadership. Jay advocates for minority student leadership, education, and professional development. Little hopes to be a beacon of change and hope for future generations of young engineers and ultimately seeks to blaze the trail and inspire more students of color to go into the field. Follow Jay on Facebook @jaylittle, Instagram @thejlittle_, and Twitter @thejaylittle.

12

MORGAN CLARKE

survival tips from experience

MY COLLEGE YEARS HAVE been the most informative years of my life. I've met some of my closest friends while in school. I've also made some of my biggest mistakes while in school.

Everything that I have experienced has taught me a lot about life, so I created a list of survival tips that I felt would be helpful.

PLAN! Everything that you do from the moment you graduate high school to the moment you walk across the stage should be planned. I personally know that if I would have taken an hour or two out of a few days of my summer to write down what I expected from myself and the university, I'd be in a much better place.

You can't just get by in college. You have to plan your classes, your eating times, your time for fun, and your time to study. It just makes life easier for you in the end.

PREPARE! Do not wait until the night before or the day of (I've done it) to write a paper. You can write one paragraph per day, one page a day, or something, but do not wait until the last minute for anything in school. Due dates arrive quickly. Anything you do in school should be done to the best of your ability. If you want things to be done correctly, you must take your time.

PRAY! Maintain your relationship with God the entire time you are in school. Don't just ask God for help when you find yourself in an interesting situation after a night out of what you considered fun. Your parents and family members are not going to be there every day to remind you to stick to your faith. You must have a relationship with God for yourself. Prayer will get you through the hard times. Prayer can keep you and your friends out of trouble and keep you out of *wrong place at the wrong time* situations. Keeping your faith while you are in school can definitely help you keep your sanity.

CONNECT! It's not always what you know, sometimes it's who you know. College is a fun time because you get to make your own decisions. That can be a double-edged sword because making the wrong decisions can have negative consequences. Building and maintaining good relationships with your dean, professors, and counselors is a must. You can do that by having a good reputation, consistently showing up for classes and meetings, and turning in your best work.

Make good decisions because your decisions determine your outcome. Let your instructors see your face! These will be the professors that write your letters of recommendation, inform you on internships, and put in a good word for you whenever you may need it. It's worth it to build the relationships.

SMALL CIRCLE! People always laugh when I say this, but I only have about five good friends outside of my sisters. I have the closest relationships with them and we each have our own special bond that makes our friendship different. It's okay to be well known, but everyone doesn't have to be your friend and everyone is not going to like you. If you have a good group of friends, you all will always encourage and motivate each other to do better. A smaller group of friends means quality relationships with people who you are invested with for life.

STAY ON YOUR PARENT'S GOOD SIDE! Your parents have always wanted the best for you. They will be there every step of the way while you're in school. Your parents are there to make sure you have everything that you need, whether it's a textbook or just to hear their voices. Parents are a great support system when you need someone to talk to.

There will be times where you have $0.40 in your bank account. Your parents will be right there to help. I can't say that I have been a broke college student. I call my parents, mostly my mom, for money bi-weekly.

BALANCE! You are basically going from asking, *What time do I need to be home* to being able to stay out all hours of the night. It's a big pill to swallow. I say that because it appears easier to play first and work later, but you need to work first and play later.

 College is fun. What will not be fun is if you are flunking out because you don't have the balance between having fun and handling business. It's okay to party on Saturday and go to class on Monday if your business is handled. If you partied on Saturday, slept on Sunday, and didn't make time to get some stuff done, you're going to be in a world of stress. Learn to have fun, but be smart about it.

GRADUATE! My university did the *look to your right, look to your left* speech where they express how everyone that you come in with you might not leave with. Believe it or not, it's true. A lot of the people that you start school with, you might not leave with. That fact alone is the reason why it's important to stay focused amongst so many distractions. Remember why you're in school and get the degree.

Morgan Clarke is a native of Grand Rapids, Michigan. She currently attends Jackson State University where she is studying Biology with a concentration in Dentistry. Morgan has three sisters and loves music and tennis. Ultimately, Morgan wants to live life as an entrepreneur and live in the South with her family. Follow Morgan on Facebook at @morganclarke and Instagram at @Celebrity_Princess

13

LEE SCOTT II

know who you are

COLLEGE IS ONE OF the most challenging, yet influential times in an individual's life. This time in life is shaped by the first level of independence and self-guidance for most of us. During this time, many people pick their majors, decide what organizations they want to get involved in, and meet their lifelong friends.

Making these decisions become your responsibility. For the first time, most of your peers are living on their own. Many become accountable for every decision, whether it's having enough money to wash clothes or which classes best fit their major and their goals. How daunting and exciting is this thought?

It becomes a lot to take on at once but it is life preparation. There are a few principles that I learned from my experience as a college student that I believe will be helpful to one's collegiate journey.

 The first principle is to find out who you are and know yourself. For many, this is the first time that you have to put in action decisions that will completely shape your college experience and life beyond undergrad. You are trying to figure out who you are. This process isn't based on who your parents or former teachers told you that you were, but who you truly are.

Maybe you were the best of the best in sports or music or whatever in high school. Well, college could be a bit of a shock. The reality is that there are other students who were the best of the best at their respective schools too. You begin to realize that you aren't the *who's who* anymore and you are starting over. Once that is gone, you may begin to really question who you are.

The best time to answer that is during your first year of college. It is normal for people to want to be accepted in some form of community. Some people can't handle the transition well, so they attempt to address this by finding their identity in the things they do or even in other people.

Everyone wants their peers to like them and embrace them for who they are. Every person has this desire to belong. This is completely normal, but you must be careful. This behavior becomes an issue if you start to find wholeness in others. If you do that, then those people will have control of your life and destiny.

I think it is an important aspect of college to get involved in positive organizations, but your involvement should never define who you are.

College is but a vapor, a twinkle in time. Your identity is important to your success as a student and life beyond college. Take time to find out who you really are, what you value, what you believe about yourself, and how you see the world around you.

The second principle is to be intentional with who you surround yourself with. If you want to be successful as a student, it would be healthy to surround yourself with successful peers. If you want to be more active and healthier, it would be a good idea to hang out with people who go to the gym quite often. Who you hang around has an impact on your success in college. This doesn't happen by accident. You must make a conscious decision to know what you want your life to look like.

The same thing happens in reverse. If you surround yourself with people who are slackers, are irresponsible, or are only in college to *turn up*, you will eventually take on some of their habits and practices. The friendships and relationships will either make you or break you.

Some relationships are by virtue of circumstance. For example, some people you might meet will be in your life at that time because of similar majors or a general education class. Maybe you live in the same dorm or have mutual friends and that is how you met. It is important to know that you can decide whether these individuals will be an asset to you or a hindrance to your success. It is necessary to see these relationships as an opportunity to grow and expand your worldview and perspective.

Throughout college, I had friends from Pakistan and Jordan, to people who grew up in my home state of Mississippi. This diversity helped me see the world in a different way and helped me grow in the pursuit of my goals and dreams. This principle helped me even to clarify what I wanted to do with my life as a career. My desire was to learn from them and how they saw the world.

Because of the diversity in my relationships, I am now able to have meaningful and intellectual conversations with the diverse group of people in my workplace about things that are happening in our world. The reason why that has worked is because of my willingness to surround myself with people who would challenge me to think from a different perspective. I could have just settled for a Mississippian or an American perspective and stayed in my red, white, and blue corner. But no, this wasn't the step I took. I was intentionally open and I'm grateful for that.

 The third and final principle is to be persistent. If you aren't prepared, college will wipe your butt. You either will drown or swim. No matter what happens, you must say to yourself that I will finish; I will accomplish this short-term goal. Believing in your abilities is important for you as a student because you will face many challenges along your journey.

Throughout school, I was a very good student in subject areas like history, English, and science, but math has been an Achilles heel. Even in college, Algebra became a thorn in my flesh. I practiced and studied. I took practice exams and would get tutors. I would consistently fall short on exams. These failures became a cycle that I couldn't seem to shake, but I made up in my mind that I was going to pass that class, no matter what it took.

I ended up taking the class two times, but I was finally able to prevail. The only reason why I could be successful is because I was persistent. I had to tell myself that it was possible for me to walk out of the class with a passing grade and move forward. For you, it may not be a class. It might be that you want to make a certain sport's roster or get into a specific club on campus.

It may not come to you easily and it may require some effort on your part to accomplish your goal, but you must keep trying. An ugly victory is still a victory. I believe that the greatest lesson you can learn about persistence is that it just doesn't stop with the last accomplishment, but it continues beyond that one great moment. These principles have helped me throughout the years and I hope that it helps you in your college experience, as well.

Lee Scott is a Jackson, MS native who hopes to inspire others to reach for their dreams and fulfill their calling. As a recent graduate of Oral Roberts University, Lee holds a degree in Leadership and plans to attend law school where he will study international law. With over five years of leadership/service experience, Lee is in the process of launching a leadership/personal development blog that will give practical tools to emerging leaders and creates a community to connect with others. Lee currently resides in Tulsa, Oklahoma where he enjoys spending time with friends, eating at the city's various restaurants and watching his favorite TV shows such as Madam Secretary, Frasier, and Parks & Recreation.

14

MARJADA TUCKER

the unwritten rules

AFTER ORIENTATION WEEK HAS ended and syllabus week (or day) becomes a blur of the past, it may quickly become apparent that everyone is not on the same playing field. Some students just seem to have everything figured out. While this is hardly ever the case (because we're all lost and/or overwhelmed at some point), understanding the unwritten rules is integral to success on any college campus. These five rules will allow a greater ease of transition and alleviate a great deal of stress in the process.

First, know your professors. Knowing your professors can be a huge benefit to you. You see them in class, but there are always opportunities to talk with them outside of the classroom. It's certainly not required that you visit your professor before or after class; however, they all share their office hours with you in the event you need to locate them.

 While it's not required, visiting your professor during his/her office hours is recommended. In fact, I suggest making it a personal requirement, even in cases where you are doing exceptionally well in a course.

The professor's office hours are not only an opportunity for you to have more personalized instruction, but that time is also an ample opportunity to connect with them as human beings.

Discussions with your professors will help them get to know you beyond your everyday assignments and projects, get letters of recommendation for graduate school and summer school programs, and can easily be the difference between an A or a B in the course. Ensure that you are open to getting to know your professors and allowing them to get to know you.

Second, you need to maintain good study habits. New material should not be met for the first time in class. If you are accustomed to studying the night before and excelling on quizzes and exams, now is not the time to stop. Skim the material beforehand (at least the night before) and highlight any areas of confusion. Reviewing the material quickly gives you an opportunity to prepare specific questions for the lecture and to actively engage therein.

As a rule of thumb, you should not feel comfortable getting behind by more than one day of material. Understand and seek mastery before moving on to the next lecture. Mastery requires constant repetition and application—there are no shortcuts.

Third, study groups, when used effectively, are the holy grail of course competency. However, they are only as effective as the individuals that comprise them. My advice is to study and work problems individually first. Then, make a list of problem areas and/or questions that you have answered incorrectly. These are the topics that should be discussed within the group.

Be mindful that each member of the group should be responsible for contributing to its success. If you are the person that must always lead the group and/or answer the questions, you are doing yourself a disservice. The underlying goal of a study group is synergy.

While it is important to read the textbook and develop a basis for learning through theory, practicing the fourth rule is even more important. Work through the problems daily. I cannot emphasize this point enough as it was one of my greatest pitfalls as a college freshman.

If you cannot teach an 8-year-old the information and answer the questions that follow, you have not mastered the information. Regurgitation of information is great until you're required to apply the concepts that you've learned to a completely different scenario.

Govern yourselves accordingly and practice active learning. Create your own problems. Understand why answers are correct and understand why the alternatives are incorrect. Whatever you do, don't just fall into the trap of aimlessly memorizing facts.

The final and fifth rule is to build a network. College is the best place to build and maintain an effective network. Avoid limiting your network to members of your own race, major, and general spheres of interest. While those connections are obviously important, focusing solely on those similarities can hinder you from making the connections that will prove critical to your success. Instead, focus on making connections that will allow you to expand your reach and enhance your skill set.

In sharing this advice, I hope that each one of you will be better prepared to meet the challenges sure to accompany this journey. Make up your mind that you will succeed. Regardless of your starting point, college is a place where you can drastically change the trajectory of your life.

If you cannot teach an 8-year-old the information and answer the questions that follow, you have not mastered the information.

Marjada Faith Tucker attends Rice University majoring in Biochemistry and Cell Biology with a minor in Medical Humanities. She is a native of Starkville, MS and was reared in the Blackjack Community. Marjada is an alumna of The MS School for Mathematics and Science where she graduated with honors and was inducted into the Hall of Fame. Marjada is proud to have been named a Ronald H. Brown Scholar, Jack Kent Cooke Scholar, Bill & Melinda Gates Millennium Scholar, Questbridge National College Match Finalist & College Prep Scholar, Philanthropic Educational Opportunity Star Recipient, and a Tom Joyner Full Ride Finalist; in fact, she was offered more than 1.5 million dollars in scholarships, grants, and awards. At Rice, Marjada is actively involved with the Minority Recruitment Committee, Black Student Association and Baptist Student Ministry. She also serves in various positions of leadership including Orientation Week Advising, First Generation Mentorship, and peer tutoring. Following the summer of her freshman year, Marjada established the Faith for P.E.A.C.E Foundation and initiated a grant funded, six-week college readiness program for Starkville youth through the local Boys & Girls Club. The following summer, she led the establishment of the Northeast Mississippi Student Leadership Conference with an underlying mission to cultivate and empower students of the Golden Triangle of Mississippi and surrounding areas. Marjada has also aided in the establishment of remote Family Medicine clinics in Grand Goave Haiti and will volunteer in Uganda in the spring of 2017.

15

AMANDA LUCAS

the five laws of academic power

THE DAYS DURING AND after your high school graduation, right before freshman orientation, are the most exciting. The feeling of anticipation consumes your entire being. It is the feeling of knowing you have a bright future that you are now solely in control of. My collegiate journey was dynamic, yet hard. I was consumed by my ego, sexuality, accolades, and a highly determine spirit to graduate. This left me with an interesting road map to offer others on what not to do. College is where you create yourself from the scraps of what you once knew to the greatness of what is yet to come. It will be glorious, but very hard and ugly work. I would like to offer five laws to help you through your freshman year and beyond.

The Five Laws of Academic Power

Law One: Remember where you came from. I went to an amazing boarding school that had truly prepared me to live on a college campus, mentally and emotionally. The morning of my leaving for my introduction to the campus, my mom woke me at four-thirty that morning.

She had to drive me three hours away to catch a recruitment bus. My mom was determined to get me there and that meant a lot to me. You see, we had no heat in the house at the time. My mother was heating the entire house with a stove.

The thought of my mother's hope and her fight to get me there, through all circumstances, not only brought tears to my eyes, but it also kept me going for the hard days to come.

Law Two: Freedom doesn't make you free. Unlike most freshmen, I didn't attend any parties off campus or participate in the binge drinking scenes you see on movies. I attended a small private liberal arts college. I felt the heavy weight of accountability resting on my shoulders, because people, including myself, had worked hard to get me there. I wasn't going to mess that up. There was no need to over indulge in any reckless behavior.

I had been making decisions on my own way before college, but witnessing the decision-making processes of my peers was more than eye opening. During these years, much of your social and academic relationships are linked together. If your social life becomes overwhelming, it can impact your academic life. Just because you have freedom doesn't mean you're free to do whatever you want. You must be responsible and work hard to make the best out of your opportunity.

Law Three: Do something you wouldn't normally do. The greatest moment in college is when you discover an untapped potential that exists inside of you. College is the perfect time to explore your potential. Not only do you have the access and resources to learn how to golf, create a documentary, do yoga, but you can also start your own business. It's the perfect time to create, fail, and start-over.

Law Four: Isolation is a no. While socializing may seem minor, having a community that you can socialize with on campus has a huge impact on your academic journey. Your key to community exist within your classmates, study groups, and lunchtime conversations. These are the relationships that will help you pass your courses, motivate you to do your best work, and network with you in the future.

Law Five: Read. Read more than you do on Snapchat, Facebook, or on *the gram*. You should read to develop a well-rounded knowledge base. What happens when you are asked to give your opinion about something? You can't google and copy and paste your response aloud. Spend less time working on the eve of deadlines and more time completing intellectual research.

 Think outside the box, explore your beliefs, and get to know who you really are and what you stand for. Perhaps you were raised to believe one thing and realize another way is more impactful. Or maybe you will discover your special ability in a subject matter or decide to work for a cause you believe in. Reading will help you broaden your horizons and open your eyes to things you may not have known existed.

College is one of the times in your life where you can create possibilities at every corner. Give yourself the opportunity to be great. Think outside the box and feed your entrepreneurial mind. Graduate to create opportunities for yourself and others. Be a mogul!

Highly motivated and driven Amanda Lucas has worked in the higher education and non-profit world for more than seven years. She is a Piney Woods and Berea College Alum. At Berea College, she received a Bachelor's degree in African and African American History. She also received the Carter G. Woodson Award, Dr. Taylor Memorial Writing Award, and was nominated for the Kennedy Center American College Theater Festival Irene Scholarship Award for the play *Amen Corner*. After Berea College Amanda graduated from Eastern Kentucky University (EKU) with a Masters in Human Services and Higher Education Student Personnel Services. Amanda has been featured in over 11 publications and written 12 articles for publications such as Town & Gown Magazine, The GRIOT, and Reader's Digest. Her recently published book: *It's Not Me It's Graduate School: Surviving Graduate School the Sassy Way* speaks to a generation of ambitious women who are caught in the depth of their academic careers and life goals.

16

ARIEL WILLINGHAM

ACT prep and dual enrollment

YES IT IS TRUE, I'm still in high school. I'm a senior this year and I am a little nervous about college even though I am excited for it. I still like living with my parents and having them take care of me. When I go to college, it is going to be very different being out on my own. Last year, I dual enrolled and took two college courses, so I was a high school student and a college student at the same time. It was cool to be able to knock out a couple of classes that I will need in college early. The advice that I want to give is about preparing for your freshman year.

The first thing I'll say is: get your mind ready for more work. When I dual enrolled, I found that the college classes required more work than my regular high school classes. Those assignments took more time and effort to complete.

It also takes more studying to pass college classes. Right now, I can get an A on a test in one of my high school subjects without even studying a whole lot. That is not going to happen with college courses because they are more intense. Studying more than one day is mandatory for college courses. On that note, stay away from procrastination.

If you are still in high school like me, I recommend you dual enrol. One of the classes I took while dual enrolling was Speech. I am very shy. The thought of taking a speaking class at all is nerve wrecking, but I was happy to be able to take it in class with all my friends instead of strangers. Dual enrolling also boosted my high school grade point average a lot.

Next, be sure to choose a college that has a good reputation for what you want to major in. Do not choose a school just because your friend is going to be there. You need to research the college choices inside and outside of your area to find the school that will work best for your needs.

 Finally, I studied hard for the ACT. I have taken it a couple of times and I did well on it, but I wanted to boost my score until I get the score that I want. Colleges will only take your highest ACT score, so it's okay to take it as many times as you want.

I started taking the ACT when I was in the 10th grade. You can take prep courses online or you can order ACT books and practice with them.

You can even take an ACT preparation class. I've done some classes, and they have really helped me. How well you learn in these classes depends on you and the teachers, so make sure to try your best. You need to do well on the ACT so that you can get scholarships that are being offered nationally, locally, or even at your school.

Do not choose a school just because your friend is going to be there. You need to research the college choices inside and outside of your area to find the school that will work best for your needs.

Ariel Willingham is a 17-year-old student at Terry High School in Terry, MS. She loves reading, painting, and photography. Academically, she is in the top 10% of her class. She is a proud Girl Scout and an active member of the Youth Media Project, where teens learn all facets of how media is produced. Her goal is to pursue a medical degree and fulfil the requirements to become a Pediatrician.

17

ASHLEY KING

debt follows you

I THOUGHT STUDENT LOANS saved me, but that couldn't be further from the truth. I'm in my senior year in college and I am already in debt. Of course, while I'm in school I don't have to pay the money I've borrowed to complete my education back, but the fact that I owe five figures is looming over my head. I will have to pay it back soon.

Debt follows you like a cloud. I'm wondering how I will ever pay this money back. But I had to get these student loans to pay for school. Not going to college is just not an option for me. I bet there are many college students out there in the same situation. There are likely many adults that have graduated from college that are making payments to student loan companies every month. It's unfortunate that you might have to go in debt just to pay for college. Sometimes grants and scholarships just aren't enough.

 During freshman year, I found out I would get refunds. That's the money left over after your grants, scholarships, and loans have paid everything. The school refunds the remaining money to you. I remember my parents telling me if I had to take the refund I should invest it back into my education. I wish now that I would have listened. It was fun over the years using that refund to party, go out of town, shop, and do everything I

didn't get to do throughout the semester. But now I realize I'm with most of America, in debt.

My advice would have to be financial in nature. Before you take a student loan, complete exhaustive research of grant and scholarship options. Only take out a loan if you must. If you don't have a choice and you must get student loans, be smart about it. Don't get more than you need, talk to your financial aid advisors and ask them not to take out loans for more money than necessary. If you do get a refund, invest it back into your education or spend it wisely. College is expensive so you must be creative and cut costs as much as you can.

Save the money to buy your books in the next semester. Sometimes, you run out of money and don't have enough to pay for books or occasionally you don't get the money in time for you to get your books early enough. You can also consider cutting costs by using a book rental company like chegg.com.

Get a summer job. Even though student loans are typically not due until you are out of college, you can make early payments.

If you get a large refund back, ask your school's financial advisor if they can return the funds to the lender. Accepting the funds obligates you to pay them back with interest.

As tempting as it may be, don't get that credit card! Run! Now that you are an adult, you will start to get all sorts of credit card offers. Throw those in the trash. Instead of focusing on what you could buy and do with all that extra money (which is really creating more debt), focus on getting a competitively high GPA that might qualify you for grants and scholarships in the coming collegiate year.

 A lot of students give up on looking for scholarships and grants while they are in college. Keep looking. There are scholarships for all types of people in all types of circumstances, not just high school seniors or freshmen.

I hope that you enjoy your freshman year. You will learn a lot about life and responsibility as you move throughout college. The choices you make in college will follow you through life. When we were younger, many of us had this right now kind of mentality. We didn't always think about the future and how our decisions might affect us. Now that we are adults, we must think and behave more responsibly. When you are making decisions, consider the impact the decision will have on your life in the long run.

Ashley King is a college senior at Jackson State University. She is currently studying Biology and focused on going to Pharmacy school. Ashley has a passion for giving back to the community and spends much of her free time doing volunteer work. You can follow her on social media @sunnybritee.

18

DAVEN SMITH

keep God first

MY EXPERIENCE IN COLLEGE was a very interesting one. I went to Prairie View A&M University in Prairie View, Texas. My freshman year was difficult because it was my first time being so far away from home. My roommates were all from Texas and I was the only Mississippian in the dorm room.

When I found out that I had three roommates, I thought it would be easy. After all, I grew up in a household with all women, my mother and two younger sisters. But, being in a dorm room with three strangers proved to be very challenging for me.

We all had different opinions and disagreed on numerous occasions. I grew up in a strict household where my mother guarded me and expected a behavior of excellence. She instilled in me to always be a lady, keep good grades, and stay pure until marriage. I heard my mother, but it all went in one ear and out of the other when I got to college.

 I got a taste of freedom from being out on my own. For a minute there, it seemed that everything I was taught growing up went out the door. I begin to party every night and skip classes. I remember calling my mother one day and asking her for money. I needed the money to buy books for class. Thankfully, she sent the money to me through a money services company the next day.

But as soon as I got the money, I went on a shopping spree. I used it to buy clothes and shoes to go party instead of buying the books I needed for class. My behavior did not reflect the values that my mom had taught me growing up.

Because of my antics and my lack of focus, I failed the first semester of my freshman year. Academic probation. That's what the letter said. If I didn't get my grades up in the following semester, the school could kick me out and give me an academic dismissal. *It just got real!*

That first semester taught me a lot. I needed to be more focused on my work, I needed to study more, and I needed to party less. I set some goals for myself in the second semester and things started to improve. It wasn't long before I realized, I was back on track. I was sure to go to class and complete my school work every day. I still partied a little, but not as much as before. I focused on my school work and stayed committed to getting good grades.

I remembered my pastor telling me before I left for college to make sure I found myself a church where my spiritual man could be fed the word of God. I looked for churches to attend. I found one in Houston, Texas. The church had a college ministry and would pick up college students on Sundays for church and feed us after the service. Everything was going great. I felt that I was on the right path spiritually, academically, and physically.

While watching television in my apartment, I began to feel a pain in my abdominal area. Then, I started to bleed. I didn't know what was wrong. It scared me. So, I caught the next flight home and went to see my doctor. I was surprised when the doctor diagnosed me with Interstitial Cystitis, which is a bladder condition. I was crushed and all I could do was cry. I just wanted my life to be better again. I was told that I would need to stay in Mississippi for medical treatment. During that time, I began to study and read the Word of God. I wanted to know what was happening to me and why. I was sad that I couldn't return to Texas to finish school. God revealed to me that I was not doing what He needed me to do in Texas and that Mississippi was where I was supposed to be for now.

 The best advice that I can give is for you to always keep God first! If you do that, God will guide you no matter what is going on in your life. You don't have to be lost and you don't have to be alone. As for me, I prayed to God to reveal what He wanted for my life and spoke to God about the desires of my heart. I spoke positive things over my life and as I continued to build my relationship with God, those things started to happen. I continued my education at Tougaloo College and I'm happy to say that, recently, I graduated.

My favorite biblical verse from the King James Version of the Holy Bible is Matthew 6:33. It says: *seek ye first the kingdom of God, and his righteousness; all these things shall be added unto you.* This verse speaks volumes to me. It says to me that if I seek after the Kingdom of God, I can have those things I speak according to His Will.

Another verse that I believe will help you is Colossians 3:2. It is found in the King James version of the Holy Bible. The verse says: *set your affection on things above, not on things of the earth.* It is my belief that when you begin to put your mind on Kingdom business and not on earthly things, you do not have time to worry about what is going on down here, because you will trust and believe that God will exceed your expectations.

According to 1 Corinthians 2:9, the King James version of the Holy Bible says: *but as it is written, eye hath not seen, nor ear heard, neither have entered into the heart of man, the things which God hath prepared for them that love him.* If you continue to stay on the path and if you trust and believe God's word, you will find that God has prepared great things for you. I'm learning that now and He has it shown it to be true in my life, every day. I pray that this will help you have a very successful freshman year.

Daven Smith was born in Gulfport, MS, to the parents of Anthony and Carrie Smith. She has lived in Collins, MS most of her life. Daven attended Piney Woods Country Life School, the only African American boarding high school in Mississippi. After her high school graduation, Daven attended Prairie View A&M University. Illness delayed her college experience; however, she later enrolled at Tougaloo College. During Daven's tenure at Tougaloo, she was member to numerous organizations. She cites her best organizational accomplishment as joining Sigma Gamma Rho Sorority during the Fall semester of 2016. Daven recently graduated Sum Cum Laude, with a Bachelor of Arts, in Child Development on May 7, 2017. She plans to attend William Carey University to work on a Masters of Teaching in Special Education, with an emphasis in Dyslexia.

19

BRYANNA BROWN

a victim of miscommunication

I STARTED AT TOUGALOO on my birthday. So, you know my first day of college was super exciting! It didn't prevent me from being a bit nervous though. This was my mom's alma mater. She attended Tougaloo College as well. Of course, just knowing that I was following in my mom's footsteps added to my excitement.

I am sort of a shy person, so with all the jumbled-up feelings I held inside, everything seemed surreal. I remember thinking that it felt like it was just yesterday that I was walking across the stage in the coliseum, collecting my high school diploma and now, today, I am starting my first day of college.

 I didn't know what to expect, but my family knew much of the staff so that put me at ease. The professors at my college were nice, patient, and caring. Many of them seemed to be laid back and calm. That perception was challenged during my very first class, Spanish. At the beginning of the school year, I had been having a few medical issues that kept me going back and forth to the hospital. As a result, I missed a few days of class. When I found out what was going on, I immediately emailed my professors to make them aware of my diagnoses and let them know when I would be returning to class.

As soon as I was able to get out of the hospital and get to the college, I went to each one of my professors, one by one, and had a conversation with each of them in regards to my absences and retrieving my missing assignments. I was successful with all of them, except one.

My Spanish professor was blunt. He said whatever came to his mind and did not seem to consider anyone else's feelings. I made several attempts to meet with him, but for some reason, he was never available. So, after all my effort, I turned to my mother for help. My mother and I met with my student success coach and, together, we came up with a way that I could receive my work without the extra hassle.

The professor wasn't happy about it. But, he finally agreed to meet with me about my work. To my surprise, he began saying that he would not accept all of my doctor's excuses. He explained to me how I should have communicated with him better at the beginning. Nearing the end of our conversation, he changed his mind and allowed me to make up all the missing assignments. I was happy about this because I knew that from that moment on, I would make up my work and put my best foot forward.

My happiness was short lived. Soon after I had gotten that resolved, my mother became ill. This time, it was worse. I took care of her until she passed away on October 25, 2016. I withdrew from school that semester to take on the responsibilities that had fallen into my lap. Wow! It had only been two months. From August to October, my life had drastically changed. It was hard after my mom passed away, but I returned in the Spring to retake my courses.

I did learn some valuable lessons during those months that I want to share with you:

1. **Communicate effectively with your professors.**
2. **Build a relationship with your professors.**
3. **Choose one of your professors to be your collegiate mentor. This would be someone who will take the time to listen to you, to give you advice, and to become hands on when you need a bit of assistance in your educational journey.**

I have found that having at least one person in your corner makes a difference. This person can help you see things from a different point of view and can help you determine the proper channels for aide, if necessary. When we go to college, we are learning more than the things that we are studying. We are learning about life. We are learning how to handle things like an adult. Although I didn't think I had an issue with communication, I took in what my professor was saying. Yes, he was blunt and seemed a bit abrasive at times, but I did learn from the experience.

If your professor agrees to be your mentor, that person will most often advocate for you and support you when necessary. You should do your part. too. No one is going to advocate for or continue to mentor someone who is not showing up appropriately in their collegiate life. So, do your best in your courses and make your professor proud. When you walk across that stage to graduate college, your mentor will hold his or her head high and be proud to call you mentee. The best part is that you will have made a lifelong friend.

Believe it or not, communication is a big part of life. How, when, and in what manner you communicate is extremely important to your professors, the staff, and even your peers. In college, no one treats you like a child. They view you as an adult. You are perceived as someone that can take care of yourself and make necessary decisions without someone holding your hand every step of the way. They try to teach you to be independent.

 What would you do if you encountered a professor who was blunt and gave you honest feedback, things that may have been difficult for you to hear? My advice to you is if you encounter someone who appears to be difficult, get to know them better. You might just find that they are not as difficult as you thought. Also, interacting with them more and showing them that you are serious about your work might open the doors to help you understand them better and give you notes on how to interact with them in a more positive way. This can start with just setting up a time and place to meet somewhere on campus and discussing anything you need to in a nice, courteous way. That's it. No strings attached.

It may also help to bring a peer or one of the other staff members along as a support person to help the communication process flow a little smoother. A mentor once told me, *if you have to constantly go to that person's office in order to get things done, then so be it. Always make sure to inform another staff member before setting up the meeting.*

When communicating through email make sure to carbon copy (cc) someone at the college in the conversation so that the professor or administrator will know that someone else such as the college president or another professor is aware of the topic being discussed. Doing this covers you in the long run whether you run into an issue or just inquiring about work, extra credit, or the due date of an assignment.

Also, try to keep a small notepad or journal. Writing down each time you visit with a professor or each time you attempt to schedule a meeting serves as documentation for your records. Take the notepad into the meeting to write down important points that are discussed. You will have those notes to refer to when you need them.

There are a million things that could go wrong when one does not communicate properly with those around them and to avoid any misunderstandings with anyone, it is better to be prepared. Always remain respectful no matter what the other person says or how they say it because if you react in the same negative way it can cause problems. It might be grounds for expulsion or it can tarnish your reputation and make your road to success harder. Please do not become a victim of miscommunication.

Bryanna Brown is an aspiring Radiologist, attending Tougaloo College. At only eighteen years old, she is majoring in Biology and getting ready for her treck to medical school. Bryanna is originally from Detroit, Michigan, but made a move to Mississippi about ten years ago. She has a goal of helping others by making a difference in their lives through medical diagnoses.

20

KENNEDY BELL

academic probation is no joke

THE TRANSITION FROM HIGH school to college was not an easy one for me. In my freshman year, I found myself on academic probation. Not at all where I thought I would end up. Imagine having to take the same courses all over again because you failed them the first time. Not only was my GPA low, but this was also a huge waste of money, having to pay for the same classes again.

Did you know that a low GPA can affect the grants you can get and you can even get kicked out of school? I knew I needed to make some changes. But how would I tell my parents?

I've had a skin disorder called Ichthyosis since birth. I often experience breakouts on my arms and on my face, which leaves a bit of scarring. Being confident is something that I've struggled with in my life because of my skin disorder. I'm shy and I've never communicated much because I don't want to draw attention to myself.   This drastically impacted my ability to ask for help when I needed it. I thought about quitting school so many times because I felt that people paid more attention to my scars, rather than me as a person.

What I learned through this journey is that if you need help, speak up. When you enter college, you are stepping into independence. You go from being a child in your parent's home to being treated like an adult on a college campus. There's not much time in between to get used to the change.

I know that if I had communicated my struggles to the advisors, my teachers, and even my parents, I could have avoided some of the failures and heartaches that I experienced. Instead, I allowed fear to overtake me and would not talk to anyone and ended up on academic probation. There was no hiding it then. When I finally did talk with my parents, they offered love, encouragement, and support, which really helped me get on a better path.

I am still shy sometimes because of my skin condition, but I know that I must continue to push forward in order to reach my goals and that's what I chose to do.

The last thing that I want to encourage you to do is choose the path that is right for you. Not everyone has to go the academic route, there are many other options that many colleges provide. I chose to take the career and technical track. The courses I take are very specific classes that prepare me for exactly what I want to do in my life. I will gain a good bit of hands on experience and knowledge and the program can even help me get job placement when I finish.

I'm not trying to convince you to take the technical route, I'm just saying to sit down and truly think about what you want to do and then choose a college experience that works better for you. There may be challenges in your freshman year, but you can get through them. Don't give up. There is no limit to what you can achieve.

Kennedy Bell was born in Jackson, MS. Before graduating from Terry High School, she participated in the Health Sciences Program at Hinds County Career and Technical Center. Kennedy enjoys helping people; therefore, after graduation, she began attending Hinds Community College to pursue a health sciences career in the Physical Therapist Assistant Program. Kennedy is very active in her local community and church. She attends St. Paul Church of God in Christ, where she is a member of the praise team, choir, and mime ministry. Kennedy expanded her quest in the workforce by breaking into the entertainment industry. She was an extra in the upcoming new feature film, *Soul Damage*.

TAMEKA DYON

the hardest class I ever took

THERE IS ALWAYS THAT one class that scares you away from taking it. It's the one class that causes a mental block. When people bring up the course name, you start shaking in your boots and having nightmares about the assignments and the grade you'll get—which of course you believe won't be an A! Listen, I'm no mathematician. I mean, I can add, subtract, and multiply but…that was the gist of it for me in college. I wasn't walking around working problems using the Pythagorean Theorem in my head or anything.

I waited to the very last possible moment to sign up for Accounting II. Okay, I guess you thought I was going to say something extremely hard, but for me, it was terrifying. Everybody's poison is different. I'd taken Accounting I online, brushed by with a B (don't know how), and just when I was about to be all *Hallelujah, Thank You Jesus* I realized it was now time for Accounting II. As a business major, this course was required, so I hankered down and decided to just get it over with.

Here's sort of how my day one went (but not exactly because I had to change the names of people and places when I wrote this). I walked into the class. It was Monday. I was scared, nervous, and literally jittery, but I managed to hobble over the other people in the class and find a seat. The professor, a short, seemingly sweet-looking lady, walked in a few minutes later. I thought to myself, *hmm…this won't be so bad. She looks nice.* She began taking attendance. But her method of checking attendance wasn't just attendance, she was doing a knowledge check.

Ms. Professor: Bryce Jenner?
Bryce: Here.
Ms. Professor: Where did you take Accounting I?
Bryce: I took it at Bryers.
Ms. Professor: Then you may want to retake it. They don't teach on nearly the scale that I do.
Bryce gave a puzzled look.
Ms. Professor: Jackie Barnes?
Jackie: Here.
Ms. Professor: Tell me about your Accounting I course.
Jackie: I was in your class last year.
Ms. Professor: Good. Andrew Nyshwaki?
Andrew: Present.
Ms. Professor: Who was your teacher in Accounting I?
Andrew: Dr. Kusack.
Ms. Professor: Dr. Brunner can't teach. Are you confident that you know the fundamentals to keep up in my class? Otherwise, I'd suggest that you drop it and retake Accounting I.

I started thinking to myself: *OMG! Don't call my name!* If she had called my name I probably wouldn't have recognized it. I was too busy thinking about what I was going to say so that she wouldn't embarrass me in front of the class.

Ms. Professor: *Tameka Dyon*
Me: *Hi.*
Ms. Professor: *Where did you take Accounting I?*
Me: *I took it online.*
Ms. Professor: *(gives me the craziest look I've ever seen) Online? No, that's not going to work. How did you do?*
Me: *I struggled, but I got a B.*
Ms. Professor: *Drop the class.*

So, while I was sitting there, feeling a bit upset and offended by her words, two students from her Accounting I class the previous term noticed the disturbed look on my face. They leaned over and started to whisper to me. These ladies encouraged me and told me not to drop the class.

They claimed that this professor was one of the best on campus and they reassured me that she would make sure I learned what I was supposed to and then some. That night, I sat at home thinking about this whole thing. *I didn't want to be in this stupid class in the first place, the professor is seemingly a butthole and not understanding, could I drop the class, was there something else I could take, but those girls said she's good…what should I do?*

Long story short, I stayed in the class. This professor was fantastic! She walked us through everything step by step and she went over concepts from Accounting I to ensure we understood. She broke things down so well, I started to love accounting and develop an interest in it. The professor wasn't mean, she was extremely nice and very patient! Quite the opposite of my initial thought.

After earning a big fat A in the class, I asked her, why the starting approach? She said she wanted the students who really cared in her class. She wanted students who were willing to put in the work. Those that heard just a bit of harsh speech and didn't want to do the work would drop or withdraw. I thought, *well that's an Interesting approach.* I was so glad I stayed.

This is my point; the hardest class is not as hard as you think. If you focus your energy and don't let the negative thoughts or the attitudes of others determine your outcome, then you can succeed.

I could have dropped the class. Truthfully, in the beginning, I was afraid. I could have come up with at least twenty reasons why I should drop. I could have let the professor's harsh words make me quit. But I didn't. I decided to stay and I got an A in the class. That was the true defining factor of my pass or fail. I didn't give up and I encourage you to do the same.

 When something seems hard, tackle it with commitment, dedication, and focus! Look at it as a challenge that you are excited to conquer and don't walk in on day one with a mindset of defeat. Think positive, do the work, and be consistent.

It may not always work out that the professor is nice, sometimes he or she might not be. It is important to remember that it's you who must get the education. The instructors have gotten theirs. Direct your focus to the things you need to do to successfully complete the class.

You really can have a great collegiate experience, if you truly want it! Cheers to the dean's list because I know you will find your way there! I know you will do great! You got this!

When something seems hard, tackle it with commitment, dedication, and focus! Look at it as a challenge that you are excited to conquer and don't walk in on day one with a mindset of defeat.

Tameka Dyon has written several books and through her publishing company she has helped others become published authors. Armed with a Master's degree in Education and a #1 best-selling book, Tameka Dyon has enlightened, entertained, and uplifted many. She has led and participated in numerous non-profit activities, community service projects, and charity events. You can follow her on Facebook at @tamekadyon.

12th grade checklist

☐ Create a support network — As a new adult you won't be able to do everything on your own. It's going to take lots of support from your parents and other trusted family members and friends. These will be the people you consult when you need to make tough decisions and need financial assistance.

☐ Create a college list — Create a list of colleges that you are interested in attending. Research each of the school's academic programs, program facilities, housing, clubs, activities, tuition, and fees.

☐ Go on a college tour — Visit the colleges on your campus list. Talk to faculty and students to find out what their experiences there are like. You can even ask to sit in on a class that you are interested in taking. Visit the cafeteria, dorm rooms, activity center, gym, auditorium, stadium, bookstore, library, career center, and tour the surrounding area to see what is in walking distance of the school. If you don't have a car, check to see what your local transportation options will be.

- Rank your college list — After you have completed your research and toured each college, rank the schools on your list. This ranking will help you determine which colleges you want to apply for and what is required of you to apply.

- ACT/SAT Scores — Take the ACT/SAT as many times as you can. Study hard to get the highest score possible. Have the testing organizations send your scores to the colleges on your ranking list.

- Recommendation Letters — Begin collecting recommendation letters from teachers, principals, counsellors, and mangers. These letters should recommend you for acceptance and tell the schools why they should choose you.

- Discuss how you will pay for college — Have an in-depth conversation with your parents about how you will pay for tuition, books, living expenses, food, and more. Develop a plan of how you will cover these items. If you need financial assistance, apply for financial aid through the colleges you selected and FAFSA. There are deadlines for these applications so research to find these out.

☐ Apply for scholarships — There are thousands of scholarships out there to help students with a variety of situations. Do your research and apply for as many scholarships as you can. This process can be very time consuming, but very helpful if you are granted scholarships.

☐ Find a mentor that is successful in your prospective major — If you are sure of what you want to major in, find a mentor who is already successful in that profession. They will be able to give you valuable advice and information to help you along your collegiate journey. If you are not sure what you want to major in, don't worry. A mentor is still recommended.

college application checklist

☐ The Application — To apply for college, you must submit an application. In many cases, a non-refundable application fee is required.

☐ Transcript — Your transcript, which includes your grades, your overall GPA, and any disciplinary records, must be sent to the college by your high school. Talk with your high school counsellor to get this accomplished.

☐ ACT/SAT Scores — Have your scores sent directly to the school of your choice. They will not take these scores from you; they must be submitted by the testing organization.

☐ Recommendation Letters — Some schools will want letters of recommendation. You can request these from your teachers, principals, close family friends, school counsellor, and/or manager of volunteer work or internship that you've completed. It would be to your benefit if anyone can speak to any of your extracurricular activities or honors work.

☐ Essays — During the application process, the college may ask you to write an essay stating why they should accept you. In addition to your heartfelt reasons, remember to list honors that you received, extracurricular activities that you were involved in, any advanced placement courses you participated in, how you measure up to others in your graduating class, volunteer work/internships/jobs that you've held, and any other special circumstances or pertinent information that may be appealing to the school.

☐ Admission Interview — Some schools require that you complete an interview before you are accepted. Some tips to help you make the best of your interview are to practice how you would answer commonly asked questions, dress appropriately, take additional recommendation letters with you, and have some knowledge about the educational institution that you hope to attend. Be sure to send a thank you note after the interview, reiterating your interest in acceptance.

dorm room checklist

Room Decor

- ☐ Alarm clock
- ☐ Lamp
- ☐ Small personal fan
- ☐ Storage bins/trays
- ☐ Bulletin board and pushpins
- ☐ Pictures and velcro or double-sided tape picture hangers
- ☐ Posters
- ☐ Items related to your hobbies
- ☐ Bed
- ☐ Comforter
- ☐ Blanket
- ☐ Pillows and pillowcases
- ☐ Sheet sets (2)
- ☐ Mattress Pad

Bath

- ☐ Hand, face, and body towels
- ☐ Shower shoes
- ☐ Bathtub mat
- ☐ Soap and soap container
- ☐ Shampoo/conditioner
- ☐ Shower cap
- ☐ Bathroom tote to transport items to the showers
- ☐ Comb and brush
- ☐ Blow dryer, flat iron
- ☐ Hairstyling products, clips, bands, etc.
- ☐ Makeup bag
- ☐ Nail bag (polish, clippers, tweezers, polish

remover)

☐ Facial bag (cleanser, moisturizer, exfoliator)

☐ Shaving bag (razors, cream)

☐ Toothbrush, paste, floss

Laundry

☐ Laundry basket
☐ Detergent
☐ Dryer sheets

Desk

☐ Television & remote
☐ PC/Laptop/Mac
☐ Headphones/earphones
☐ Small speakers
☐ Game station & controllers
☐ DVD/Blu-ray player
☐ USB flash drive
☐ Memory card
☐ Pens and pencils
☐ Notebooks
☐ Folders
☐ Backpack
☐ Dry Erase Board, markers, and eraser
☐ Calendar
☐ Index cards

Cords

☐ HDMI, DVI, Ethernet
☐ Surge protector

- ☐ Extension cords
- ☐ Chargers

Kitchen Items

- ☐ Small refrigerator
- ☐ A couple of plates, bowls, cups, and utensils
- ☐ Foil, plastic sandwich bags, covered containers
- ☐ Paper towels
- ☐ Wet wipes
- ☐ Dish soap and dish towel
- ☐ Microwave

Clothing

- ☐ Pants/shorts
- ☐ Shirts, sweaters
- ☐ Underwear
- ☐ Pajamas & housecoat
- ☐ Active wear
- ☐ Lounging wear
- ☐ Shoes, boots
- ☐ Jacket, coat
- ☐ Cold weather wear
- ☐ Hats
- ☐ Business-casual clothing
- ☐ Swimwear
- ☐ Shades
- ☐ Jewelry

Household Items

- ☐ Cleaners

Grown & Gone

- ☐ Tissue
- ☐ Lightbulbs
- ☐ Can opener
- ☐ Trash bags
- ☐ Batteries
- ☐ Flashlight
- ☐ Air freshener

grown & gone challenge

Challenge! You are in college and this is the beginning of the full life that you have ahead of you! That said, it's okay to step outside of the box and create positive opportunities for yourself.

- ☐ Travel abroad — When summer comes, use your time wisely. A few years of college may seem like a lot, but it won't be long before you are working in your career and trudging through your day to day responsibilities. So, why not travel abroad? Look into your school's study abroad program and consider participating.

- ☐ Take a few fun electives — There will be an opportunity to take some classes that have nothing to do with your major or the program requirements. These classes are typically called electives. Here's your opportunity to explore some things that you never thought about doing or that you've been interested in but never had the chance to experience. You are paying for these courses, so why not check out a few fun classes like drama, tennis, photography, dancing, swimming, or another course of your choice. Either way, be sure to talk to your counselor before you sign up for any fun classes.

☐ Take an internship — You are getting your education to work in the career of your choosing, but how can you get experience to keep yourself competitive after you graduate? Internships. Internships will allow you the opportunity to work for a major company, in a position associated with your career choice, where you can learn, learn, learn. The advantage is that you get on the job training, something you may not get in college. Also, you are building your resume, showing that you learned more than theory through your collegiate years. Be mindful that there is no salary with some internships.

- Go to summer school — Why not get ahead and graduate early. During the summer, you can take one to two courses, depending on the school, to push you ahead with your credits.

- Take a fun group trip — You've made a lot of great relationships with people in college and you've established your core group of friends. Maybe there are four of you and you've got about three months or so to have fun. Why not travel? This plan works perfectly if each of you live in different states. Take a few weeks to spend time at each person's home, one after the other. It gives you an opportunity to get to know your new friends better and helps you travel the world.

contribute to part II

Thanks for reading! Read more for your chance to be a part of Grown & Gone II. Please add a short review to let us know which story/tip/checklist helped you the most!

When the idea of this book came to me, I was excited to bring the project to life. From the very beginning, I wanted this to be a collaborative project where freshmen and soon to be freshmen could get real world experience from people around their own age. I felt strongly about having college students and recent graduates be a part of this project because I knew that they would have a unique perspective into the struggles of a first-year college student.

As you've read, the number of mistakes and mishaps that can happen in your first year run the gamut. Does this book mean that you will have these exact things happen to you? No. Does it mean that this is all you need to worry about? No. Should you do exactly what this book tells you to do because this is the only way to handle these scenarios? No. Are there likely many other things that we could have talked about in this book? Yes. There will likely be other ways that you can address some of the things that we went through, and maybe your methods will work out better for you. To that same note, you are sure to encounter some issues that we didn't discuss. Of course, we couldn't cover every topic in this book, but what we did was try to offer you open and honest information based on our own life experiences in the hopes that it could help in some way. Hopefully, this book will save you from a couple of mistakes in your first year of college. And, if you have already made the same or similar mistake, now you know you are not alone.

Getting input from the contributors was amazing and funny, at times. Especially when we talked about the name of the book and what it should be. My thought was a survival guide for college students or something of the sort, but they felt strongly about the name Grown &Gone. Many of them polled other students to see which name they felt was best, and surprisingly, Grown & Gone got the most votes. It took a little bit of coercing, but I eventually gave in to the idea. Just as the students explained it to me, it describes exactly what stage of your life you are in, as a freshman.

Another reason this project is important to me is because I also have a personal goal of increasing the number of young adult authors in the world. I believe that writing helps to break down communication barriers and gives people the opportunity to share their experiences with a wider audience. An author's words can truly have a positive impact on someone else's life.

As a college student, becoming an author can set you apart from the rest. Let's imagine that your major is forensic science and your book on DNA testing is published. When you graduate college and you are being interviewed for your first job, you've got an edge over other recent graduates. Writing a book about a topic related to your industry shows passion for the area that you're pursuing. Imagine going in for an interview and telling them that you are a published author. Instant resume booster!

If you are interested in writing a book and getting published like the contributors in this book, I can surely help you. I am also working on the second phase of Grown & Gone to add additional stories and tips from more students. If you are interested in being a part of that project or writing your own book, contact me at www.ilpublications.com. You can also send us a review or words of encouragement for future readers that might make the second book. Use the contact page on www.ilpublictions.com.

Ultimately, we hope our stories and tips, along with the handy checklists, will be helpful in your first independent year of college. We would be so thankful if you would, please share a review of which part of the book you feel will help or has helped you the most so others know the value of it. Good luck and congratulations on taking your first step – heading into college! Yes, this is really happening! Ah, the college life! It's your freshman year and you are, officially, grown and gone!

encouragement central

In addition to stories and tips from the contributors, take a few minutes to read what we are calling encouragement central. You will find that the world is just as great as you thought it was. Outside your front door are millions of people that want to see you succeed. We posted a call to action on Facebook from people who wanted to send encouraging words for you during your freshman year.

It's okay to be afraid, but just don't let fear
hold you back.
--James Williams

One of the most essential keys is knowing
and understanding you are capable of
anything. Don't second guess your
greatness.
 --Steven Thomas

Be blessed and be a blessing.
--Bobby Willis

Birds fly because they believe they can. You
can succeed too if you believe you can.
--Russell Myers

Be obsessed or be average.
--Jamey Jenkins

Always stay a student. Be willing to continuously learn!
~~Stacie Sherriff

Listen. You might hear something that'll help you get to where you're trying to go. Nobody knows everything.
~~Michael Jones

If there's no ambition, then there's no vision.
~~Gerold Girbeau

Focus. Don't be afraid to take chances.
~~Shenetha James

Put God first and you will succeed.
~~Diane Wallace

Your inner circle of friends is paramount to your success! Just because you have history, they are cool, or you owe them something doesn't mean that they should automatically qualify. Choose wisely.
~~Breyon Bradford

Don't rush. Don't fear. Just accomplish, taking one day at a time. Above all, put your trust in God.
~~James Wilson

If you fall, dust yourself off and get back up. Keep going!
~~Tameka Dyon

Everyone's heart beats, but few beat with purpose.
~~Bilal Qizilbash

Never let anyone convince you that your dreams aren't valid just because they don't understand them. Your dreams do matter!
~~Monica Sheree

The brightest light you should ever allow to shine is your inner light. Greatness lies within you!
~~Markita N. Barnett

Never let fear allow you to forget that you are confident enough to succeed.
~~Elizabeth Gonzalez

Pray for wisdown, guidance, and revelation of your purpose.
~~Mieyatta Malone

Whereever your focus is, your actions will follow! Cautiously choose your direction of travel.
--Floyd Patterson

The key to moving on is to forgive.
--Charde Denise

Do not reject the pushing to your greatness, that means that somebody cares about you and your future
--Gigi Gates

At the end of the day, where you sacrifice is where you will succeed.
--Reginal Bronson

If you just try, things that seem unreachable will become surprisingly reachable.
--Taneja Dyon

Don't judge the value of your life achievements based on those around you.
~~Shakina Cooley

Don't dwell on the failures or the shortcomings of achieving your dreams, just realized you're birthed with something greater that the world hasn't yet seen.
~~Tamarah Mack

Acknowledge when you don't understand something connected to being a successful college student. Befriend the right people, ask detailed questions, and move when you are clear on next steps to success.
~~Tonja Murphy

Put in work for what you want.
~~Shenetha James

Do not chase jobs/career for money. Chase jobs/careers that bring you fulfillment. When you find the job that you love, the money, accolades, and perks will follow.
--Bobby Willis

Everyone is not your friend, but your true friends will be like the roots on a tree. They will find you. You won't have to look for them.
--Xavier Smith

If you have not given your life to Christ, then do so. You will need His guidance the more you become successful.
--Christopher Wheatley

Stay focused. Everything will work out if its meant to be.
--Shenetha James

When you set out to do things better than those before you have ever done, you get to a place where you are broken and fell all hope is gone, look to the arms of the Father and know that you are not alone.
~~Michael Harris

Stay focused and believe in God first. Trust in Him and He won't let you down.
~~Todd Johnson

Keep educating yourself. Control your emotions. Be grateful.
~~Keisha Mallard-Martinez

Dreams are what you make them!
~~Galean James

Shine your light and inspire!
~~Steven Thomas

You don't have the option to be mediocre. Be present and do more, out pace your competition, and help your teammates. And when you can't do anymore, do some more.
~~DaMond Davis

Have faith. Believe in Yourself. Take action in achieving your dreams.
~~Keisha Mallard-Martinez

Climb the ladder to success. Be careful at every step you take to make sure you don't slip off.
~~Victor D. Willis

Success is getting back up and giving it one more try.
~~Chris Carson

Make sure whatever you do isn't just for money. Make your venture something you enjoy, after all, you will be spending half of your life doing it.
--AJ Iredale

Remain steadfast in your beliefs and know that you can do anything with God's grace and help.
--James Cooper

Once you've found your niche, master it!
--Steven Thomas

Stay focused and plant the seed of determination in your mind.
--Larry Dunnell Edwards

You don't need a crowd so choose your friends wisely.
--Diane Wallace

Failure is a key factor to success. Never let it keep you from success.
--Cortdarrel Strong

Walking in your divine greatness will inspire others to walk in their greatness.
--Mieyatta Malone

Always keep your eye on the ultimate prize, but be kind and compassionate along the way.
--Tom Ricks

Let your major and your God given gifts mesh. Put your head to the plow and move forward with purpose!
--Floyd Patterson

acknowledgements

There are so many people to thank for this project! This section was not edited. It was written the way that the students wanted it.

Keyaira – I would like to thank all my mentors, close friends, and family for never giving up on me! For always preaching and instilling in me that God has a plan for me, and that with Him anything is possible. Thank you so much for accepting me and all my flaws and showing me that everything that I went through was necessary in the development of the woman I am today. Most importantly I want to give the highest praise and honor to God for NEVER leaving my side and for continuously guiding me & molding me into the person he knew I could be. I was also blessed with these amazing people: my pastor, Reverend Dr. Casey Fisher, my mentors, Michele Fisher, Toni-Lowe Fisher, Ebony Gardner, and Wanda Bell, my mother, Lashonda Jackson, my father, Terrell Chiplin, my cousins, Ashlee Percy and Ann Jenkins, my aunt, Carla Jackson, and my amazing friends, Keishondra Fisher, Mikayla Colston, Breanna Lynch, Aleeshah Smith, Carlisa Jenkins, and Angel Rhodes. These are people who

have made such an impact on my life whether they know it or not. I love you so much and thanks for being there for me when I needed y'all the most!

Morgan – I'd like to take the time out to thank all my family and friends that have supported me on my journey into adulthood. I especially want to thank my mother for always being my main supporter and my go to. There have been a lot of people that have taken the time to pour into me and I have taken every bit of advice. I would like to thank God for giving me the tools to be successful continuously and for the people He's put in my life. Thank you! Rhonda Clarke, Anthony Johnson, Louise and John Clarke, Joshua and Hilliard family, Susie Gibson, Amy Broekhuizen, Bishop and my Lighthouse FLC family, Kyah, Meg, P, Paige.

Amanda – To the Piney Woods School for your hard work when it comes to preparing students for the world of academics. More than 90% of students just like me go on to college. I thank you for instilling in me the values of academic promise for a future of intellectual freedom. For you and all you do.

Marjada – I am eternally grateful to God for entrusting me with a platform of leadership and empowerment. To my mother, familial support system, mentors, and friends who have encouraged me continuously on this journey, I would like to express my sincerest thanks. I would also like to formally acknowledge the foundations, individuals, and organizations that have invested in my future and given me an opportunity to obtain a college education.

Xavier – I just want to thank God because He makes all things possible and He is moving in my life in all ways. I also want to thank my mother for always being in my corner and for being my support system in everything that I have ever done.

Adesuwa – My father, Dr. Stephen I.N. Ekunwe, for teaching me how to be

passionate and pursue excellence.

Jasmine – First off, I would like to thank God! Without Him, there's no telling where I would be. I'd like to thank my parents, Leon and Erica Whipps, my sister and brother, Jaye and LJ, my family, my godparents, Mark & Tracey Scott, Tala White, and Walter Halbert, my many sisters and brothers (it's too many of y'all to name), my church family, Greater Peace International Ministries, and my loving fiancé, Thaddeus Macklin.

A'mya – I would like to thank my grandmother and parents for always believing in me, even when I didn't believe in myself.

Elizabeth – I would like to take the time to acknowledge the support of my beautiful family that includes my parents: Bertha Gonzalez and Joel Gonzalez; and my siblings: Jocelyne, Jennifer, and Joel. Additionally, I would love to give a huge shout-out to Dr. Stevie Dawn Blakely for being a great mentor and devotee. Thank you all for being the fuel that I need to get things done. Los amo mucho! Furthermore, I want to express my deepest gratitude to Tameka Dyon and the individuals involved in launching Grown & Gone. I am ecstatic to be a part of the team!

Mercedes – I would like to thank God for allowing me to be able to create, and receive so many opportunities to inspire others.

Ariel – I would like to thank God and my parents. Thank you, mom, for letting me be a part of this project. I love you.

Ashley – I would like to thank my parents and my grandparents. You all have always inspired me to be the best I can be. Thank you, mom, for pushing me to participate in this. Thank you, dad, for believing that I will change the world one day. Because of that, I will always strive to make you proud.

Charde – I would like to thank my family for always being there for me, even when I pushed them away. I would also like to thank Alex for being a best friend

and more. You lifted me up and brought me out of my downfall. Last, but definitely not least, I would like to thank God. If it wasn't for Him, I wouldn't have these special people in my life and I certainly wouldn't be where I am today. I love you all! Thank you.

Daven – I would like to thank Jesus Christ for paving a way for me to be here today. Also, I would like to thank my mother and my sisters for always supporting me no matter what I choose in life to do. You were always there for me. Thank you, Carrie Smith, Danielle Smith, and D'Angela Smith.

Bryanna – Thank you mom, Shena Brown, for everything. I would also like to thank Ya'Sarrius Lowe and many more.

Kyle – I would like to take this opportunity to first give honor to God for the opportunity to share my gift of writing with others. Huge thank you to Ms. Tameka Dyon for imparting this vision and providing young writers a platform to showcase their abilities. Thank you to my beautiful

Mother and Grandmother, Angellee Kidd and Angela Shaw for being tough on me for a purpose growing up as it relates to my writing and public speaking skills. I can't thank you both enough for constantly instilling in me the rewards of hard work, prayer life, and being consistent in the pursuit towards success. Thank you to Jackson State University and the School of Journalism and Media Studies for also providing tools needed to be a successful journalist in such a competitive industry. If I have forgotten your name, charge it to my head and not my heart. I am appreciative of everyone that has given wisdom, advice, prayer, and even tough love. I cannot say thank you enough!

MarKie'Sha – I would like to first thank God for blessing me with such influential and supportive people in my life. My mother is my ROCK, I would like to thank her for her patience, support, and love over the years. I would also like to thank my family for being supportive and helping me to develop into the young woman I am today. My high school English and science teachers have

been important to my development also, with their diligent and effective styles of teaching. Last but not least, I would like to thank my mentors that are there at the most awkward times to help. I don't think people understand the importance of supporting others unselfishly. it is the efforts of many people, family, friends and colleagues that help people develop into well rounded individuals.

Tameka – One of the best parts of writing this book was sitting down with the contributors and putting this project together. Without them, I never could have captured the stories and tips that were given to make this book valuable. Thank you to all of you. I think any time you write about your life, you're never sure if it's going to be interesting or of use to anyone else, so thank you all for your bravery. I was blessed to have people that inspired me along the way: Lamont Khian Facco, James W., Esaw, Ida, Kenneth, Edgar, Valerie, James K., Ashley, Ariel, Tiffany, Brianna, JJ, Brayden, Nicholas, Kenyatta, Jamie K., Wilbur,

Dyon, Kapree, Mekhi, Gigi,
Stacy, Tonja, Taunya,
Nozipo, Jahmal, Justin,
Monica, and Ardrena.

Made in the USA
Coppell, TX
22 October 2021

64493099R00103